Stanley Leathes

The gospel its own witness

The Hulsean lectures for 1873

Stanley Leathes

The gospel its own witness
The Hulsean lectures for 1873

ISBN/EAN: 9783337282448

Printed in Europe, USA, Canada, Australia, Japan

Cover: Foto ©Thomas Meinert / pixelio.de

More available books at **www.hansebooks.com**

THE GOSPEL

ITS OWN WITNESS.

THE HULSEAN LECTURES FOR 1873.

BY THE

Rev. STANLEY LEATHES, M.A.,

MINISTER OF ST. PHILIP'S, REGENT STREET;
PROFESSOR OF HEBREW, KING'S COLLEGE, LONDON.

Henry S. King & Co.,
65 Cornhill, and 12 Paternoster Row, London.
1874.

PREFACE.

By the changes of recent years the Hulsean Lectures have been reduced from twenty to eight, and from eight to four. The limit of four lectures is manifestly too narrow for the detailed discussion of any important subject or the development of an elaborate argument; and the fact of the vacation being selected as the time for their delivery, —as was the case with the present lectures, which were appointed for the last two Sundays in Lent, Good Friday, and Easter Day, when, for the most part, there could be no congregation,—is not more favourable. It was therefore thought advisable to address one's self as directly as possible to the main object of the foundation, namely, the evidential aspect of the Christian faith, in a plain matter-of-fact, common-sense way. If what was written was to have any wider publicity than the small circle of immediate hearers, the more popular it could be made the better.

There is a prejudice often felt against speaking of Christianity in the character of an advocate. Christianity, it is assumed, needs no advocacy. This may be very true, and Christianity does indeed desire nothing but a fair field and no favour. But we may question whether, under all circumstances, to show it no favour, or at least no personal interest, is to secure it a fair field. It is as impossible at once to believe and to disbelieve as it is to like and to dislike. If we really believe that Christianity bears the mark of a Divine origin, then we cannot be so impartial as to regard it as merely human. There is a philosophic treatment of Christianity which may be consistent with being a Christian, and Christianity is or may be the highest philosophy; but it is also possible to lose the Christian in the philosopher, and the bearing of the disciple in that of the impartial judge. If we are forbidden to be advocates and required to be judges, it is too often forgotten that Christianity itself requires us to be disciples. If, however, we are sincere disciples we need not shrink from being advocates likewise, so long as we do not suffer our advocacy to warp our judgment.

In the following lectures, which, though for 1873 were delivered in 1874, there are many points that obviously might receive, if indeed they do not require, more lengthened treatment; but the main drift of the argument, so far as it aims at being one, is, I hope, sufficiently clear and alike independent of such treatment and deserving the attention of earnest inquirers and of thoughtful students.

CONTENTS.

I.
THE WANT IMPLIED BY THE PRESENT ASPECT OF THE CHURCH 1

II.
THE PRIMITIVE GOSPEL 45

III.
THE EFFECTS OF THE PRIMITIVE GOSPEL ... 89

IV.
THE REGENERATIVE POWER OF THE GOSPEL 135

THE WANT IMPLIED BY THE PRESENT ASPECT OF THE CHURCH.

ROMANS i. 3, 4.

Concerning His Son Jesus Christ our Lord, which was made of the seed of David according to the flesh; and declared to be the Son of God with power, according to the spirit of holiness, by the resurrection from the dead.

THIS is the statement which St. Paul makes of that gospel which he desired so earnestly to proclaim at Rome. It is very simple, very definite, and very full. It is, conspicuously, a gospel of fact rather than of doctrine, a personal rather than a dogmatic gospel. There may indeed have been many points which the great teacher himself would have regarded as essential to the integrity of his message which are not expressed even if they are implied in it; but it is scarcely possible to conceive that he would have been willing to surrender any one of those points which are here explicitly enumerated. The reality of the Divine Sonship of Jesus; the fact of His personal descent from the family of David; the validity of His claim to be the promised Messiah, which was intimately connected with this fact; the historic truth of His resurrection from the dead; the unblemished holiness which was at once so characteristic of His life, and so needful to be followed after by every one who named His name,—these, we may presume, were, one and all, integral and indispensable elements in the professedly Divine message which he bore.

Nor is it possible to call in question the authoritative character of this statement as a summary of the earliest Christian teaching. In its most literal acceptation it is not at variance, but in striking harmony, with the testimony even of the synoptical gospels. In them we are taught, in no ambiguous manner, the Divine Sonship of Jesus, His royal lineage, His claim to be the Messiah, the fact of His resurrection, the holiness of His personal character, the holiness He required of His followers. It cannot be alleged thus far that the teaching of St. Paul was different from that of Jesus or of the earliest records of the life of Jesus; while the genuineness of the epistle itself rests upon a basis of certainty, and its declarations on these and similar matters are capable of the fullest corroboration from other productions of the same writer equally indubitable. We have, moreover, from one of these productions, the Epistle to the Galatians, the most emphatic assertion on the part of the writer himself of the permanence and unchangeable character of the message which he proclaimed.[1] In the face of these reiterated

---

[1] Gal. i. 8, 9.

assertions it cannot even be pretended that in the opinion of the writer himself the message he was so anxious to deliver was liable to substantial modification, still less to material change. He may indeed, not unnaturally, have been somewhat over-sensitive about the perpetuation of teaching which he regarded in some sense as peculiarly his own; but as to what his opinion was on this matter, there is no shadow or sort of doubt. He considered what he termed his gospel to be of such a nature that not even the proclamation of an angel from heaven could suffice to set it aside, and yet more, he believed that when its message had been adequately received, it could not be reversed even if he were himself to declare it false.

And looking at this matter in the light of the present day, the question naturally arises, how far the apostle was justified in his opinion, and how far we ourselves are bound by it. That his opinion adequately and accurately represented the first utterances of the gospel, as far as we have any means of ascertaining them, there can be no question ; the only question is, how far that gospel was itself independent of those utterances, and capable of being improved.

Some thirty years ago this question was not without general interest to the Church, from the bearing which it naturally had upon the controversy with Rome. It was then felt, and the course of subsequent events has fully justified the feeling, that the letter of Scripture alone was not sufficient as a basis for Roman teaching. The authority of tradition and the theory of development were openly invoked to its aid. The first expression of Christian doctrine was not complete, but germinal. The seed was sown, but the plant, the flower, and the fruit were its natural and necessary after-growth. What has been one obvious result of the adoption of such a theory is perfectly well known to all of us. Its actual success has probably far exceeded the most sanguine anticipations of its originator.

But a reaction unavoidably ensued. There appears to be that Teutonic element in the English character which is in hopeless antagonism to the usurpations of Rome. The claims of the Church were unendurable, even if the final authority of Scripture was not recognised. And now there has arisen another difficulty from a totally opposite quarter. The former premises being adopted, a very different conclusion has been arrived at. The insufficiency of Scripture has been assumed in order to make way for the claims of reason, and the greater development and the freer exercise of the critical faculty. The tendency now is to believe that the gospel-revelation is superannuated, that mankind has outgrown the teaching of apostles and the doctrines of Christianity, that our only hope is in the unrestrained progress of the intellect, and the unfettered license of speculation. The natural passion for freedom rebels against the thought of being held in check by the utterances even of a Paul or John. They were not only men of like passions with ourselves, but of weaker and less mature judgment than we, and their recorded opinions are to be taken only for what they are worth, and must be allowed to stand or fall solely upon their own merits. Thus the pure gospel must be carefully and critically distinguished from St. Paul's one-sided and biassed enunciation of it.

Many influences have combined to produce this condition of thought and feeling, or an approximation to it. The triumphs achieved by the pursuit of the inductive method in physical science have naturally led men to believe that there should be no limits to its employment, although the precept and example of its first and greatest master were alike opposed to its intrusion into matters of Divine faith. The rash and precipitate conclusions which have oftentimes been adopted in the name of criticism, which have obtained the greater notoriety from being the more audacious; a love of theory, and a disposition to generalise hastily, rather than patiently investigate facts, or recognise the true bearing of facts already established; a thirst for novelty, together with the spirit of general restlessness and dissatisfaction with former results, however sound, which is a characteristic of the age we live in—these, and similar tendencies, the force of which we must all more or less acknowledge, have conspired to bring about a general unsettlement of mind upon subjects which, if of any, can only be of paramount, importance.

Nor is the present position of parties within the Church itself, or the general aspect of other prominent Christian bodies, calculated to produce a favourable impression upon the mind which judges from without. There is a want of real unity, and the apparent presence of any principle of cohesion among members of the same Church. The intense earnestness of personal piety, which more than half a century ago was not without conspicuous examples here and elsewhere, is not so manifest now. Those who occupy the same relative position in the sphere of theological opinion, by no means fill the same place. There is, moreover, in these cases an inability to sympathise with many of the questions which agitate inquiring minds, that renders them ineffectual as guides for the perplexed. They are apt to confound walking in the old paths with a repetition of the old phraseology and the utterance of former watchwords, without any reference to the changed aspect of things, and the modified requirements thereby superinduced. Truth, though it must always be in essence one, is various and manifold in its outward form. It is difficult to stereotype the expression of truth and retain at the same time its spiritual freedom and elasticity; but nothing surely is more requisite than this in the conflict of truth with many-sided error. The arms and armour of mediæval warfare would be worse than useless in the battles of to-day. If, therefore, we would offer an effectual resistance to the foe we have to grapple with, it can only be by trying to understand his position and seeking to appreciate his strength. The modern representatives of that school of thought which was the salvation of the Church in the commencement of the present century can scarcely be said to have aspired to do this.

Moreover, notwithstanding their great numerical strength, it is very doubtful whether they must not yield, in point of increasing influence as well as numbers, to another and more recent school, who claim to be the truest representatives of the original and undivided national Church. Here, however, also there appears to be for the most part a want of appreciation of the present phases of our position, and of its truest needs. The central life of Christianity is confounded as it seems with allegiance to some very subordinate standing order, and devotion to a rubric or a service-book is apparently regarded as of greater importance than the moral influence of Christian teaching on the heart. The channels of salvation in sacraments and ordinances appear to be too often identified with the salvation itself—the stream of living water with the mechanical contrivance through which it flows. There can be no question as to the popularity of this section and its teaching. If success or usefulness is to be measured by adherence, by attachment and obedience to a system, there should be no question as to the greatness of its work done. It is one of the most striking features of Christianity, that its influence can predominate over the defects of system, that its fragrance escapes from the casket in which it is enshrined. Still, it is only too manifest that the eagerness to enlist sympathisers with one particular direction of what is called Church feeling, is much stronger than the desire to maintain those particular elements of Christian faith which are common to other and diverse members of the Christian body. The zeal, for example, which is displayed to uphold the doctrine of Baptismal Regeneration, or the Apostolical Succession, is greater than any which is felt for the truth of the Messiahship of Jesus, or the reality of His resurrection from the dead. It is of course assumed that these are points already acknowledged and received, whereas the others are, it may be, less securely established; but still one must admit that the degree of interest manifested in these and similar points is in the inverse ratio to their essential importance. For example, it stands to reason that the reality of the death of Christ must be a matter of greater moment than the doctrine of the Real Presence in the Eucharist, and yet the degree of interest manifested in maintaining the latter is greater than any that would be displayed in defence of the former ; or to put it otherwise, more sympathy would be felt with those who accepted the doctrine of the Real Presence than with any who had a profound conviction of the reality and virtue of our Lord's death. It is, however, obvious that, without pronouncing any judgment on the doctrine of the Real Presence, the reality and virtue of the Lord's death must be more essential to the life of Christianity, and, consequently, ought to be able to elicit among Christians a proportionately greater amount of interest. If, therefore, in any one section of the Church points of subordinate or external interest are regarded with the greatest favour as symbols of union and occasions for sympathy, there must surely be reason to fear that it is because the points of more central and vital interest are less appreciated as bonds of union, if even they are not held with less tenacity. It is only too evident that, unless this section of the Church can be brought to estimate the present position of the Christian faith in its relation to the thought and feeling of the present day, it must fail signally in its witness for Christ before men, because, being necessarily but partial and limited in its aspect of truth, it cannot hope to convey the whole truth to others. It is something more than a revival of mediæval customs and mediæval methods of thought that is wanted in the struggle of to-day; it is the reproduction of that very life which underlay those customs and modes of thought, and which can no more be identified with them than they can be with the earliest expressions of the Christian life.

There is, however, another and a popular and increasing section of the Church in this land which demands our attention. It is comprised of those who, having been educated in one or other of these earlier sections, have broken loose from either or from both, in righteous indignation against the narrowness which characterised them. It was felt that Christianity must be something more than belief in or allegiance to the verbal inspiration of a book, that it could not be bound for better or for worse to a particular phase of teaching, which was created by the accidental attitude of Romanism on the one side, and of Protestant Christianity on the other. The logic of facts and the open message of nature had a claim to be recognised as well as traditional reverence for the Word of God and the intentionally cautious formularies, or the elaborately vague decisions of the Prayer-book. The absolutely final character of a declaration of faith that was put forth three centuries ago, was not only regarded as arbitrary and anachronistic, but was felt to be inconsistent also with the very principles to which its own origin was due. The Church of the sixteenth century had no prerogative by which it was authorised to legislate absolutely for the Church of the nineteenth. Other interests were afloat, and other questions were mooted; other aspirations were awakened, and other difficulties were felt, which lay altogether beyond the ken of the reformers, and for dealing with which, therefore, they could not be accepted as authoritative, still less as infallible guides. The attitude of those who felt thus was essentially a protestant attitude. Their reverence for the past might be great, but their reverence for common sense, for reason and for truth, was greater. They felt, moreover, that the National Church was to be a reality, and not a name, and that therefore it must be able, more or less, to sympathise with, and adapt itself to, the altered condition of the nation.

It is impossible not to see that there is much

of truth in such convictions, and that there is probably a more lively sense of the real want of our age in this section of the Church than in either of the others. It may be questioned, however, to what extent we may implicitly trust its guidance. There is something inherently vague in a programme which is arranged mainly by the prevailing taste or requirements of the hour. What we really want more than anything else is some abiding principle. If popular taste and not principle becomes the ruling influence, we have manifestly no guarantee that the decisions of to-day may not be reversed to-morrow. The exigencies of the passing hour may be very urgent, but there are others that will outweigh them. If conduct is to be governed by circumstance and not by principle, it must necessarily be vacillating and inconsistent. And there are not wanting evidences of this in the most recent phase of religious thought in the Church. There is a tendency to be chiefly swayed by the latest manifestation of popular opinion, whatever that may be. The boundary line of definite belief is a movable limit which may be shifted according to expediency or to pressure. There is no one opinion which may be regarded as fixed or certain. All must be considered as liable to change. Even the most widely-received beliefs are to be held only as provisionally true; true, that is, till they are believed false—till, in fact, they have been outvoted, and the majority have declared against them. What if among such beliefs should be the substantial historic truth of the Gospels, the fact of our Lord's death, the reality of His resurrection, the actual mission of the Holy Ghost, the essential difference between natural and revealed religion, or the like. It is manifest that in that case there must be an end to the teaching function of the Church, because she would have nothing certain to teach; she would have nothing to give, because there would be nothing that she had received.

Now, in the face of these diverse schools and tendencies, which are so conspicuous in the religious thought of our day, what are we to choose, and how are we to act? It is difficult, if not impossible, to sympathise altogether with any. And yet surely there is much that must command the sympathy of the sincere Christian in all. The depth of earnestness and zeal in one, the exceptional and laborious activity of another, the breadth of thought and large-hearted liberality of a third. What is requisite for the perfect man is doubtless a fusion of their several qualities, rather than a choosing between them. And we cannot doubt that the religious instinct of the future will require something more than the preservation or revival of one or other of these various modes of thought. The natural law of change which governs everything in this world will dominate also here. The change which has passed over one of these sections in the last forty years is very conspicuous. Starting from a platform mainly of dogma, it has become chiefly zealous about ritual. When its first pulpit utterances were marked by a chastened purity and severe simplicity of style, the preaching which is most in vogue now affects or emulates the impassioned fervour, not to say the rant, of uneducated nonconformity. Its most attractive form in the present day appears to be an unctuous sacramentalism, which has borrowed largely from the accidents and the language of the revivalistic camp-meeting, offering in this respect the greatest possible contrast to its earlier and more ostensibly orthodox manifestations. The religious taste, even within the confines of rigid ecclesiasticism, has suffered change.

In the other direction of so-called liberal thought this is no less conspicuous. The transition from the early sermons of Arnold to the corresponding productions of the same school in the present day, is very marked and very wide. The disciples of Robertson have gone much farther than he went. The tendency is manifestly to surrender yet more. The hold upon distinctive elements of Christian truth is much less. There appears to be a desire to break loose from everything which can impose restraint, and to begin the search after truth *de novo*, as if there had been no continuity of Christian teaching from the first, as if the gospel had never been preached or written, as if the kingdoms of the Roman empire had not long ago become the kingdoms of the Christ.

Nor is it possible, even if it were desirable, to arrest this tendency to change, this impulse which results in progress. The attempt to do so would be in the highest degree revolutionary; nay, more, it would be doing violence to nature. The question, however, which inevitably suggests itself is, if religious thought and sentiment are so liable to change, what reason have we to believe that everything which can be called Christian thought will not become altogether a thing of the past? If Christianity is simply a matter of the opinion, it seems impossible but that it should be so. One very popular phase of teaching in the present day professes to concern itself almost exclusively with the morality of the gospel. Consenting to regard all opinions as possibly false, none as more than probably true, it takes refuge from this general vagueness and uncertainty of thought in what is supposed to be the secure and indestructible bulwark of morality which is common to every form of Christianity, and, at the same time, independent of any. Manifestly, however, this is virtually to surrender all Christian belief as inherently weak and untenable, to regard none as worthy of being made a rallying point, or becoming a centre of union and a ground for united action.

Now, whatever may be the abstract merits or demerits of such a position, one thing at least is clear—that it differs *toto cœlo* from the earliest manifestations of Christian teaching. There was no vagueness or uncertainty in them. Taking the four great epistles of St. Paul as specimens, we have inculcated there a moral code of unrivalled purity and wisdom. But prominent as the morality doubtless is, it nowhere occupies the first place. It is built upon a foundation, not of opinion, but of fact. It does not appear to have been foremost even in the apostle's mind. It is postponed to the announcement of something else. It is deduced from it. And that from which it is deduced is declared by him to be of permanent and unchangeable importance. There can scarcely be a greater contrast than between his position and that which so many are disposed to assume in the present day. The only question is, Which is the true one?

Unquestionably the greatest possible injustice is done to Christianity when it is represented or tacitly assumed to be a matter chiefly of opinions, a religion principally of beliefs. And yet this is the way in which the three great sections of the Church in this country are disposed to regard it. The elder section, which glories in evangelical traditions, is zealous for some scheme of salvation, an arrangement with which all the facts of history and of life, and all the varieties of personal character and disposition, are expected to be made to square. The well-known programme of ruin, redemption, and regeneration is conceived of as a panacea of infallible efficacy, which no spiritual disorder, however complicated, can resist. If the attempt to administer it uniformly and at all hazards excites loathing and nausea, it is never for one moment surmised that there can be anything wrong but in the patient. The prescription is one of established and unquestionable repute. But surely if any such formula is an adequate expression of Christianity, it can only, or must chiefly, be regarded as a religion of sentiments and opinions. The facts which were the keystone of apostolic teaching have here become diluted into and identified with a set of congealed and crystallised notions about the facts. The person of the dying and the living Lord has disappeared in some theory as to what He did. A stereotyped impression of certain consequences has usurped the place of the original and energising cause. It is obvious that faith in the living virtue of the cause must be weak in proportion to the obstinacy with which we cling to some one theory of its mode of operation. Truth is always greater than our thoughts about it. We can never with safety confound the two.

But assuredly such observations apply with even greater justice to those who are chiefly devoted to some insignificant and external item of priestly dress, or ritual observance, or doctrinal minutiæ. The belief in seven sacraments is regarded as a matter of more vital import than the authenticity of the fourth gospel. The celebration of that which was originally known as the Lord's Supper is considered a heinous enormity at any hour later than noon. The expediency or necessity of Auricular Confession is more eagerly contended for than the reality of the new life in Christ. But it can hardly escape any person of discernment that there is here altogether a different tone of thought from that which is found in the Epistle to the Romans, or in the Sermon on the Mount. The two lines may have been identical once, but they are divergent now. A religion of facts and moral precepts and spiritual influences has become one of opinions and observances. The central figure of the breathing Christ is concealed by a mass of accessories and drapery. The actual reality of the Person has been forgotten in the provision that has been made for keeping Him in remembrance. Simplicity has been swallowed up by systematised routine. There is a long interval between the religion which thus expresses itself, and that which we perceive in the Acts of the Apostles. And the difference is one which is no doubt felt.

But then again with those who are chiefly anxious to adapt traditional Christianity to the thought and practice of the age, there is even a stronger tendency to represent it only as a matter of opinion. It is openly asserted that there is little or no connection between faith and fact. The historic occurrence of events recorded in the gospels is but timidly affirmed, perhaps but partially believed. The present is regarded as the sufficient measure of all the past. The commonest actions of life are thought to have in them so much of the Divine, that it is a mistake to seek for true Divinity elsewhere. Humanity itself is a thing so sacred, that we want no object of worship higher than that which is truly human. Nature in her infinite manifestations is a power so holy, that it were vain to imagine any power beyond nature could be more so. What is most essential is to make the Bible speak the language of nature and of common sense. So long as it fails to do this its truest power is not felt. The electric telegraph and the steam engine are as much works of the Spirit of God as turning water into wine or raising the dead. There is no difference in kind between the inspiration of a Shelley and the prophetic rapture of an Isaiah. The circumstances of the two being changed, the phenomena presented might have proved convertible. Emotional religion is held to be so treacherous and delusive, that to pray without one particle of feeling is adopted as the correct type of prayer, and to work for the mere sake of working as the highest ideal of life. To suppose, therefore, that truth is anything more than opinion to which the force of circumstances impels us, is impossible. It must inevitably change with the changing hour, and consequently to dispense with everything like conviction is the safest and the wisest course. To take the world as we find it, and make the best of it, is all that we can do. It were alike absurd and futile to preach any gospel to this age in the belief that it came with any heavenly sanction, or was endowed with any specially Divine virtue. Christianity itself, in its earliest form, was but a mixed and defective system, and it rests with mankind at large to supply its deficiencies and to purge it of all impurity. The progressive instincts of the race may be safely trusted to do this, and it will be done.

Now, it cannot be denied that we hear the echoes of such thoughts as these in various quarters. They are becoming more or less characteristic of a growing party in the Church. As little can it be denied that they are in strong contrast to the whole tenor of the New Testament. Indeed, it is secretly felt, if not openly confessed, that the teaching of the gospels and epistles must be conformed to the age, and not the age, with its accessions of strength and vast influx of light, to the teaching of half-educated apostles and illiterate evangelists. And it is quite as well, nay, it is absolutely necessary, that we should deliberately face such thoughts and sentiments, in order that we may clearly understand our own position. How are we prepared to act, and with whom are we disposed to side? It is sufficiently obvious that there is no one section of the Church that is entitled to demand our unqualified allegiance. There are blots and deficiencies patent enough everywhere. Will it be wise, however, to become impatient with the perplexities confronting us, and despair altogether of the Christian cause? Surely not. The very object for which we appear to be placed in a world of trial, perplexity, and temptation, is that we may learn to refuse the evil and to choose the good. It is impossible, under any circumstances, to escape from this responsibility. Neither does the fact of our position in the Christian Church secure our immunity therefrom. It is the object of Christianity to kindle a bright light within the heart by which we may be enabled to discriminate between truth and falsehood, good and evil, and even the several forms of Christianity cannot claim to be exempt from the necessity for the application of this power.

The lesson, therefore, to be derived from the confusions and divisions of the present day, is the lesson of discrimination and of combination. We have to separate the dross from the gold, and to combine the better elements of every section.

There is the warmth of a genial humanity in the one, the strength of a Divine faith in another, and the practical wisdom of common sense in a third. Why should they not be all united? Is there any other way in which we can adequately represent the measure of the stature of the fulness of Christ? It is only by combining the qualities of length and breadth and depth and height that we can obtain the just proportions of the solid cube. If any one proportion is sacrificed to any other, the perfection of the whole must suffer. And it is certain that in every case that which can alone supply the requisite fulness and solidity, is a firmer and more comprehensive grasp of the central facts of the Christian faith. The condition of thought within and without the Church is a witness that we want a gospel; but if so, it must be a gospel of fact and not of opinion. It is too much forgotten that Christianity rests on facts, appeals to facts, and is essentially a religion of facts. It is either because sentiments have been substituted for facts, or doctrines have been considered as equivalent to facts, or facts have been regarded only as the expression of ideas, that the development of error in one direction or the other has prevailed. And in like manner it is only by placing the facts of Christianity in their right relation to sentiments, doctrines, and ideas, that our position can be rectified or our condition improved. We must endeavour to distinguish between the facts which are inseparable from the religion and the opinions which are incidental to the facts. In this way we shall not only discover a remedy for our various defects, but shall also render our Christianity more real and healthy.

Again, it is not by the exaggeration of individual peculiarities that men can be drawn together, but by the development of those qualities and dispositions which they possess in common; not by magnifying points of difference, but by seizing and making the most of points of sympathy. And in the midst of the divisions of Christendom, and the state of religious thought in our own Church, the common facts of the Christian faith, however they may have been forgotten, are such points of sympathy. To invest them with their true importance is to find in them rallying points of union. To recognise their deep significance is to feel their essential vitality, and to be quickened by their life.

On the other hand, it cannot be doubted that the prevalent tendency to regard Christianity as a religion rather of opinions than of facts, has reacted with a pernicious influence on the facts themselves. The opinions have been opposed and rejected on abstract grounds, and their rejection has occasioned a prejudice against the facts. If it had not been for the opinions with which the facts had been conventionally associated, it may be doubted whether they would have excited any more suspicion than other traditionally received facts. But as it is the two have been rejected together.

It is certain, however, from the opening of the Epistle to the Romans, for example, that the first promulgation of the gospel was that of a series of facts connected with a person. It concerned Jesus Christ our Lord, who was born of a certain family, who died and rose again from the dead. It cannot be pretended that the results which followed on the first preaching of the gospel were produced in any other way. Such a theory would be directly in the face of the evidence. Certain facts were proclaimed, and certain results followed their proclamation. Believers were the more added to the Lord,—multitudes both of men and women,—and by degrees the world became converted.

And it is surely not too much to suppose that analogous results would follow the proclamation of the same facts now. If there were more earnest faith in the historic reality of our Lord's Life and Death and Resurrection, if these events were grasped by the mind as the real occurrences of yesterday, there would be the less tendency to translate them into the rigid and frigid metaphysical dogmas with which they are so often regarded as identical. If the spiritual nature and reality of the Ascension, and the mission of the Holy Ghost, were more vividly apprehended, there would be less devotion to the externals and carnal ordinances, which are too frequently mistaken for communion with the Spirit. Nor would it be possible to confound the human and the Divine, the holy and the secular, as some are prone to do. Christianity is a religion of facts and not of notions, it fades and languishes when notions are allowed to usurp the place of facts. It recovers itself and revives when the truth and majesty of its facts is adequately asserted. The results which followed the first preaching of the gospel are found by experience to follow it now. The human heart acknowledges the power of the facts, and surrenders itself to Him of whom they are proclaimed. That such facts, whatever may have been their explanation, should, upon their proclamation eighteen centuries ago, have been followed by certain definite results, is perhaps not altogether surprising; but that identically the same power should be found to characterise their proclamation now, and that the same results should be produced, or be capable of being produced thereby, is, to say the least, sufficiently remarkable. And the significance of this fact, for fact it is, must be regarded as by no means the slightest evidence that the gospel of the Life and Death and Resurrection of Jesus is, as the apostle in his own case had found it to be, nothing less than the power of God unto salvation.

The existing state of the Church, then, in its

division and confusion, may be regarded as a witness to the need of a power which is, somehow or other, lacking, but which the gospel professes to supply. In what does that power consist, and where is it to be found? The Church professes to have and to hold the doctrine of salvation, and yet withal is not saved. If the prominent ideas of salvation are those of healing and wholeness, then it is only too evident that the Church is not saved. In an imperfect condition, such as ours, it is not indeed to be expected that any ideal should be completely realised. In the individual life of the Church there may be, and doubtless is, much of that vitality which her corporate existence fails to show; but still it is to be desired that the whole body should be saved as well as some of the members. And we may wisely and earnestly inquire whether there is any healing of her wound, and in what way she may be made whole. Such a question is suggested to us both by the rejection of Christianity on the one hand, and by the divided aspect it presents on the other. Those who reject it declare plainly that they want something which they fail to find in it, though they find it not elsewhere, while no one type of Christian teaching can be considered as altogether satisfactory. In what direction, then, are we to seek for the remedy which we feel we want? Is it by breaking loose from all the past and sallying forth in quest of something new? or is it by returning to first principles, to the ancient types of Christian life, and seeking, not indeed to reproduce their form, but to imbibe their spirit. If the primitive gospel, as it is stereotyped for us in the earliest records, is indeed from God, then it is probable that we shall find in that the remedy which we want. If it is not, we shall of course search for it there in vain. But if upon inquiring we find, not only that it professes to supply our need, but appears to be likewise constituted to do so, then we may surely arrive at the conclusion that a gospel which professes to bring salvation, and appears also to be fraught with it, is indeed not a cunningly devised fable of man's invention, but the very message and method of the living God, which He has designed for the healing of the nations. If it appears that there is that in it which can still give life to the soul, and that if we are not saved it is because we have not received it as the message of life, then will the Gospel be found its own Witness, and the fact that in the light of God we see light, the surest proof that it is a good and perfect gift derived from the Father of Lights, with whom is no variableness, neither shadow of turning.

There is surely need in these days for such convictions to live and to die by. We are fast losing our hold on this life, fast drawing nigh to the eternal judgment of the next. It is worth while inquiring seriously how we stand with regard to another world and another life; whether we have any sure and certain hope of one to come; and if so, upon what grounds. The gospel of Jesus Christ professes to have the promise of such a hope as nothing else has. We cannot escape the responsibility which our moral constitution lays upon us of being judges of the gospel claims. We must decide, each one for himself, whether or not the gospel of Jesus Christ is the authoritative expression of the will of God, and by that decision we must abide, not only in the full flow of vigorous life and unsolicitous ease, but in the solemn moments of our helpless and final struggle with death. But that of which God has constituted us responsible judges will eventually become our judge, and by its decision we must abide. For conscience itself bears witness to the reasonableness and the truth of our blessed Lord's assertion: "He that rejecteth me, and receiveth not my words, hath one that judgeth him : the word that I have spoken, the same shall judge him in the last day." [1]

[1] Her Majesty's Judges of the Lent Assize were present at the delivery of this lecture.

II.

THE PRIMITIVE GOSPEL.

THE PRIMITIVE GOSPEL.

St. Mark i. 1.

The beginning of the gospel of Jesus Christ, the Son of God.

THE question, What is the gospel? is one which must often have been suggested to our minds, not only by the study of Church history, but also by the actual phenomena presented to us by the existing phases of religious life and the attitude of religious parties. It is a question which, if answered at all, can only be answered by an appeal to the records of the New Testament. Whatever may have been the origin of the four gospels, there can be little doubt that each was intended, in some sense at any rate, to be a sufficient expression of that which appears from the first to have been understood by "the gospel." For example, St. Mark's object in writing must have been to convey to his readers, whoever they were, an intelligible idea of what he himself called "the gospel."

It would manifestly be a very long inquiry to examine the whole of the New Testament for an answer to the question; but if this remark is in any degree just, we may conclude that an answer, not altogether inadequate, may be obtained by taking any one of the four gospels at hazard and making that the field of our inquiry. Let us, then, take the Gospel of St. Mark, and see whether, supposing we possessed no other record, it would be possible to gather from it any clear ideas of what the writer and his readers alike must have understood by "the gospel."

He commences in this very abrupt and enigmatical way: "The beginning of the gospel of

Jesus Christ, the Son of God." The subject-matter of his treatise, then, is "the gospel," and it is itself apparently designated as a gospel. This double use of the expression, familiar to us now, must have been as early as the time when the evangelist first wrote. The book is rightly termed a gospel: the subject of it is the gospel.

Again, it is the gospel of Jesus Christ that he begins to write. It was a narrative, then, about a particular person, and not about himself. It nowhere appears from the narrative who the writer was, so completely is his individuality lost. The narrative also is not only about a particular person, but is in some sense his gospel, —the gospel which he brings, and for which he is responsible. This very shortly appears as the narrative proceeds.

The person is called, without introduction, Jesus Christ,—the readers manifestly being supposed to be familiar with His name, which, however, was partly Greek and partly Jewish; though indeed the part which was Greek was expressive of ideas wholly Jewish. This person, moreover, is called the Son of God; according to our present notions a somewhat ambiguous title, but one which to the mind of a Greek must have suggested an origin other than human, and which to the mind of a Jew must have implied yet more. The narrative probably will tend to unfold more definitely the sense in which the writer applied this title.

Abruptly, however, as the so-called "gospel of Jesus Christ, the Son of God" is introduced, it appears to be implied that it was not altogether new, but that preparation had been made for it. Reference is made to the writings of the prophets, and it is assumed that the readers are familiar with them. They must have had, therefore, at any rate to a certain extent, a Jewish education; they must have known and accepted the sacred books of the Jews. They seem to have believed that the latest of these books had spoken of the advent of this person four centuries before, and one of them at least seven centuries and a half. This is entirely independent of what *our* notion of the authorship of these books may be, and is simply a matter of fact as regards the obvious opinion of the writer and his readers. Both alike manifestly believed in the existence of ancient prophecy, and its office as an indicator of the coming gospel. For in the prophets it had been declared, that a person should come before whose face a messenger should be sent to prepare the way for him. This messenger, we are given to understand, was John, who, it was remembered, did baptise in the wilderness, and was the author of a remarkable religious movement which had been attended with great success. He had announced himself as the forerunner of One who was much greater than he, and who should baptise with the Holy Ghost. In this hairy man, who did eat locusts and wild honey, it is clear that the evangelist recognised the messenger of the Lord of Hosts, the Son of God, whose coming had been foretold. Whatever our opinions may be, either on the subject of prophecy or of John's movement, it is absolutely certain that this is what the evangelist believed, and what he desired those for whom he wrote to believe also.

The coming of Jesus, therefore, had been prepared for in two ways. Many centuries before it had formed the subject of prophecy; and for a few weeks or months (the exact time does not appear) the preaching and remarkable career of John, as well as his distinct testimony, had created in men's minds an expectation of some one who was about to come, and who, when he came, should have extraordinary spiritual powers at his command, to which the preacher himself laid no claim. This fact was the more remarkable because the extraordinary movement of John was what, in the common parlance of our own day, would be called spiritual.

Such, according to St. Mark, or at least the second evangelist, was the beginning of the gospel; a beginning which extended from his own time, or at least from times within his own recollection, far backwards for many hundred years.

Before, then, we have heard a single incident of the Christ, we have been surrounded with the machinery of the supernatural and the spiritual. It is not needful to define these terms more minutely, because the definite prophecy of an event centuries before it occurred answers to what is popularly understood by supernatural,—it cannot be explained on merely scientific or natural principles, however on such principles it may be explained away; and however we may interpret the phrase "the Holy Ghost," it is clear the writer used it very much as it is now popularly used. To multiply definitions and to split hairs on such matters is practically to darken counsel by words without knowledge. The writer clearly expected to be understood without further definition on his part, and consequently may be supposed to need it not on ours; added to which his language, fairly and attentively considered, sufficiently interprets itself.

The person spoken of as Jesus Christ is said to have come from Nazareth of Galilee to be baptised of John in Jordan. He is forthwith proclaimed by a voice from heaven to be the Son of God. So that the first introduction of Jesus compels us to regard Him as in immediate relation to the Divine being. The voice at His baptism is clearly introduced to illustrate the mysterious title bestowed upon Him from the first. Let it be remembered that we are simply inquiring now into the nature of the primitive gospel as it was proclaimed by one of the four gospels, deducing our evidence about it from that alone.

We are next briefly informed that Jesus was forty days in the wilderness tempted of Satan; that He was with the wild beasts, but was, we may presume, uninjured of them; and that the angels ministered unto Him. Here it would be very desirable to know more, but we are not told it. We are not even told the issue of this temptation, we are only led to infer it; still less are we told its nature. The Son of God is able to assert dominion over the wild beasts and the evil spirit—He has angels at His command, but is not exempt from the temptations of humanity. As the mission of John was in some way connected with the introduction of Jesus, so His baptism by the preacher appears to be connected with His temptation in the wilderness, and that again with the inauguration of His own ministry. Jesus, we are told, returned into Galilee and began to preach the gospel of the kingdom of God, which He announced as at hand, because the time was fulfilled. It is difficult not only to understand the terms in which Jesus first announced His gospel, but also to determine the exact ideas which must have been derived from its announcement. The phrase, kingdom of God, appears without any comment or explanation, and the only clue we have to its meaning is furnished by the words of Daniel ii. 44 : "And in the days of these kings," that is of the fourth, or Roman, empire, "shall the God of heaven set up a kingdom, which shall never be destroyed : and the kingdom shall not be left to other people, but it shall break in pieces and consume all these kingdoms, and it shall stand for ever" (cf. vii. 14). It would seem that Jesus must have expressly referred to this passage, for otherwise we are at a loss to understand what notion those who heard Him could have derived from His words. It is evident, however, that

He considered repentance, or a change of mind of some kind, an essential pre-requisite to the advent of this kingdom, and that its advent was dependent on belief in the gospel. Not more perplexing and remarkable, however, was the announcement of Jesus, than was the success which immediately began to attend it. He sees two fishers plying their occupation on the sea of Galilee, invites them to come after Him, and promises to make them fishers of men ; whereupon, strange to say, they immediately forsake their nets and follow Him, and shortly afterwards others do the same. Now, we must bear in mind that thus far there is nothing, properly speaking, miraculous, or which can be rejected therefore on that account. We are consequently bound, without prejudice, to accept the narrative as simple history; and yet at the same time it is in the highest degree unaccountable. Strange it is that Jesus should have acted as He did ; stranger still that He should have met with the success He met with; and yet we have no valid cause to doubt either. From the first, then, there is something altogether beyond the ordinary course of events in the career of this mysterious person.

The next incident recorded is not less singular. He enters a synagogue and preaches, which one would suppose He had legally no right to do, though custom had given Him a prescriptive right. But the most conspicuous success instantaneously attends His efforts. He is at once recognised as a powerful and altogether original teacher, and the people are astonished at His doctrine.[1] There can be no question, therefore, that from the first the movement which Jesus originated was strictly what we should term religious, and in no degree political. His announcement of His gospel; His invitation to Simon and Andrew; and His choice of the synagogue and the Sabbath day as the

[1] Mark i. 21, 22.

place and time to teach, are sufficient proofs of this.

We now come, in St. Mark's Gospel, to the first of a series of some eighteen or twenty miracles which are circumstantially described as being wrought by Jesus, and may be classified thus : Four of them are cases of demoniacal possession ; five of healing disease ; three of controlling nature ; two of giving sight to the blind ; two of feeding great multitudes ; one of curing a deaf and dumb man ; and one of raising the dead. These have probably been selected by the evangelist out of many more for a particular purpose, and they seem to show that the power was attributed to Jesus of curing what may generically if not specifically be termed madness, of healing various diseases, such as fever, leprosy, paralysis, and the like ; of controlling inanimate nature, as, for example, by stilling the tempest, walking on the water, killing the fig-tree by a word ;

of giving sight, and speech, and hearing where these faculties were impaired or lacking; of sustaining great masses of people with food in the desert; and of restoring life to the dead. We are given to understand that the cases specified are only samples of what was habitually done by Jesus; and therefore it must be observed that, if in one or two cases we may suppose the persons witnessing the miracles to have been deceived, this is not sufficient to account for all of them, their diversity and wide range of subject being an additional element of difficulty in accounting for them. We are at all events at liberty to say that the primitive gospel attributed to Jesus the mastery over nature, the control of the human spirit, and the dominion of the realms of health and sense, and life and death. We are not now concerned to account for this belief, but only to record it. If one tithe of such works were actually performed by Jesus, then we need inquire no further into His instantaneous power over His diciples; while, if there was any truth in His first declaration, that the kingdom of God was at hand, and any fitness in the character He from the first assumed, even such mighty works are rendered partly intelligible.

If such, then, were the characteristics of the person whom the primitive gospel proclaimed, it is more important for us to determine what they would then have been understood to imply than what explanation we can give of them; for it is only by understanding them as they were then understood that we can form a just estimate of the person of Jesus according to the evangelist; and there can be but little doubt how they would then have been understood.

The next traits we meet with in St. Mark are the statements that Jesus rose up long before daybreak and departed into a solitary place to pray;[1] that He associated with publicans and

[1] Mark i. 35.

sinners,[1] and declared that the *Son of man* was lord of the Sabbath-day.[2] This remarkable phrase, which has only once before been used by St. Mark in the narrative of the paralytic,[3] and is used some five times afterwards, is clearly convertible with the phrase "Son of God," which was used in the opening verse of the first chapter. In healing the paralytic, it was also understood that Jesus laid claim to the power of forgiving sins. Subsequently we are told that unclean spirits when they saw Him fell down before Him and cried, saying, "Thou art the Son of God."[4]

Again, He goeth up into a mountain and calleth unto Him whom He would, and they come unto Him as before. Of these He ordains twelve, and delegates to them the marvellous powers possessed by Himself, and is thought by His friends to be beside Himself.[5]

---

[1] Mark ii. 15.   [2] ii. 28.   [3] ii. 10.
[4] iii. 11.   [5] iii. 13—21.

We are next presented with a sample of the teaching of Jesus, which was to a great extent by parables, but five of which, however, are recorded by St. Mark. The first of these singularly represents to us the conception which Jesus had formed of His own work. He was a sower sowing his seed,[1] which to a great degree was fruitless; but where it succeeded was eminently fruitful. This parable was an apt illustration of what, as a matter of fact, Jesus did. He communicated to mankind germinal truth. He invented no system. He promulgated no theory. He founded no elaborate organisation. But He proclaimed truth, which was to be like seed, to take root, to expand, to grow, to bring forth fruit, to multiply. Nothing can express more accurately the moral work of Jesus than this parable of the sower. Two other parables are immediately added, which bear upon this one, and are spoken to illustrate the nature

---

[1] Mark iv. 3.

of the kingdom of God, which was the first burden of His teaching; that, namely, of the spontaneous and gradual growth of seed,[1] and that of the grain of mustard seed,[2] both of which exhibit the same or similar characteristics of His moral teaching. It is clear from these parables that Jesus anticipated the most extensive and successful results from His teaching. The actual effects of the preaching of the gospel during eighteen centuries cannot be said to be greater than these anticipations would seem to have been. There can be no doubt that He intended to produce the very extensive results which have followed from His moral teaching.

The following instances may serve as specimens of what the teaching of Jesus was as it is preserved to us by St. Mark, omitting that which is involved in the parables and the miracles. When His disciples were asked why it was that

[1] Mark iv. 26. [2] iv. 31.

He ate and drank with publicans and sinners, He replied that it was the sick only who had need of the physician :[1] showing thereby the estimate He had formed of His own work and office; and when asked why His disciples did not fast like those of John and the Pharisees, He virtually implied that man's condition was such that fasting was inadequate to mend it; that patching the old bottles would not suffice to keep the new wine, but that the bottles must be made new to hold the wine;[2] showing the estimate He had formed of that nature which He came to heal, and of His own ability to heal it. On the occasion of the scribes alleging that His mighty works were done by the power of Satan, He showed the impossibility of that power being exercised to its own detriment, and the consequent unreasonableness of their allegation, pointing out at the same time the guilt of those who wilfully confounded the

---

[1] Mark ii. 17.   [2] ii. 21, 22.

origin of the works of light and darkness, and would not discriminate between the two.[1] Being told that His mother and His brethren were seeking for Him, He replied that whosoever should do the will of God was His brother, and sister, and mother.[2] He also took occasion to affirm the absolute worthlessness of all external acts without the spirit of true worship, when some of His disciples were reproached for eating with unwashen hands, and showed the natural tendency thereof, observing, for once at least, with bitter irony, "*Full well* ye reject the commandment of God, that ye may keep your own tradition;" and showing also that the source of moral depravity was the heart of man.

The importance which Jesus attached to faith, and the pains He took to inculcate it upon His disciples, are seen in many ways. It was when He "saw their faith" that He said to the paralytic,

[1] Mark iii. 23. [2] iii. 35. [3] vii. 9—23.

"Son, thy sins be forgiven thee."[1] It was when His disciples were alarmed at the storm of wind on the sea, that He said unto them, "How is it that ye have no faith?"[2] To the woman with an issue of blood He said, "Daughter, thy faith hath made thee whole."[3] To the ruler of the synagogue He said, "Be not afraid, only believe."[4] In His own country it is even implied that the faithlessness of the people operated as an impediment to His doing any mighty work, for it is said that "He marvelled because of their unbelief."[5] When His disciples were troubled at seeing Him walking on the sea, He said, "Be of good cheer: it is I; be not afraid,"[6] which must be compared with the corresponding incident mentioned before. It was the disciples' want of faith that was implicitly rebuked when He said to them, "Why reason ye because ye have no bread?"[7] for

[1] Mark ii. 5.   [2] iv. 40.   [3] v. 34.   [4] v. 36.
[5] vi. 6.   [6] vi. 50.   [7] viii. 17.

He reminded them of the two former occasions, when He had fed five thousand and four thousand with a few loaves. With apparent reference to His disciples He said, in reply to the father of the demoniac, "O faithless generation, how long shall I be with you?" and afterwards, "If thou canst believe, all things are possible to him that believeth."[1] To blind Bartimæus He said, "Go thy way; thy faith hath made thee whole."[2] The lesson which He inculcated upon Peter and the rest from the withering of the fig-tree was, "Have faith in God:" assuring them that mountains even should be removed by faith, and saying, "What things soever ye desire, when ye pray, believe that ye receive them, and ye shall have them."[3]

It is to be observed that in all these cases faith cannot, by any possibility, be understood of an intellectual belief in dogma : it is not any pro-

[1] Mark ix. 19, 23. [2] x. 52. [3] xi. 22, 24.

position or doctrine that is implied as the subject-matter of belief, but rather that relation of person to person, and of heart to heart which is expressed by trust. It is implicit and direct trust or confidence in God, or reliance on the personal goodness of Christ, that is illustrated and enjoined. It is belief in the spiritual power of the man Jesus, and the relation subsisting between that living person and the invisible God, that is implied and commended, that state of the inner man by which he is enabled to receive and perceive the grace and goodness of God. "Thy faith hath made thee whole" could not mean that the tenacity with which he had retained certain articles of an intellectual creed had made him whole, because there is no clue by which any such creed can be discovered, but that the strong confidence and entire self-surrender with which he had cast himself on the mercy of Jesus of Nazareth, in whom he had recognised the son of David, his clear perception and devout acknowledgment of Him, his personal trust in and reliance on Him, had made him whole. This is certainly the natural inference from the literal teaching of the record of the evangelist. This is the kind of spirit which would be developed by the study of the examples presented by him. The first readers of his narrative would naturally learn this from it, or at least they might do so.

It is desirable to inquire, moreover, what it was that Jesus taught His disciples and others about Himself. We read that when the unclean spirits fell down before Him, and cried, saying, "Thou art the Son of God," He straitly charged them that they should not make Him known.[1] But when His disciples were astonished at the sudden calm which followed His rebuking of the wind and the sea, they exclaimed, "What manner of *man* is this, that even the wind and the sea

[1] Mark iii. 12.

obey Him?"[1] The demoniac, on the contrary, out of whom Legion was cast, was bidden to go home to his friends, and tell them how great things the *Lord* had done for him, and, says the writer, "he departed, and began to publish in Decapolis how great things *Jesus* had done for him."[2] On one occasion, and one only, we find Him asking His disciples whom men said He was, whereupon when several answers had been given, he again asked, "But whom say ye that I am?" and when Peter replied, "Thou art the Christ," He charged them that they should tell no man of Him,[3] manifestly implying that Peter's answer was correct. Now it was, we are told, that He *began* to teach His disciples that the Son of man must suffer and die, and rise again.[4] In the same chapter He speaks also of the Son of man coming in the glory of His Father with the holy angels.[5] After His transfiguration He charged

---

[1] Mark iv. 41.   [2] v. 20.   [3] viii. 30.   [4] viii. 31.   [5] viii. 38.

His disciples that they should tell no man what things they had seen, till the Son of man was risen from the dead: a saying, however, which they did not understand.[1] Again, we are told in the same chapter, that He taught His disciples, and said unto them, "The Son of man is delivered into the hands of men, and they shall kill Him, and after that He is killed He shall rise the third day. But they understood not that saying, and were afraid to ask Him."[2] Again, as they were in the way going up to Jerusalem, He began to tell them *what* things would happen unto Him more minutely, saying, "The Son of man shall be delivered unto the chief priests, and unto the scribes; and they shall condemn Him to death, and shall deliver Him to the Gentiles: and they shall mock Him, and shall scourge Him, and shall spit upon Him, and shall kill Him: and the third day He shall rise again;"[3] and, afterwards,

---

[1] Mark ix. 10. [2] ix. 32. [3] x. 33, 34.

He enjoins humility upon His disciples, "for," He says, "the Son of man came not to be ministered unto, but to minister, and to give His life a ransom for many."[1] This, then, is the fifth distinct allusion He has already made to the circumstances of His own death.[2] He has also, four times, spoken distinctly of His resurrection,[3] and has once implied His ascension and His return in glory to judgment.[4] Beside this, in the parable of the vineyard and the husbandmen, spoken at Jerusalem, He very plainly intimated His own death;[5] and, in the house of Simon the leper, He spoke of the woman who anointed His head as having come beforehand to anoint His body to the burying.[6] Shortly afterwards we are told that He made His disciples very sorrowful by saying that one of them should betray Him.[7] Again, He declares that His death is imminent,

---

[1] Mark x. 45. [2] viii. 31; ix. 9, 31; x. 32, 45.
[3] viii. 31; ix. 9, 31; x. 34. [4] viii. 38; cf. xiv. 62. [5] xii. 8.
[6] xiv. 8. [7] xiv. 18, 19.

and speaks for the fifth time of His resurrection.[1] He foretells also the threefold denial of Peter.[2] At the Last Supper, the same evening, He "took bread, and blessed, and brake it, and gave to them, and said, Take, eat: this is my body;" and of the cup which He gave to them, after He had given thanks, He said, "This is my blood of the new testament, which is shed for many," and intimated that He was drinking of it for the last time.[3] It appears to have been at this supper, or about the same time, that He began to teach His disciples that He was the subject of prophecy: "The Son of man," He said, "indeed goeth, *as it is written of Him*."[4] "All ye shall be offended because of me this night: *for it is written*, I will smite the shepherd, and the sheep shall be scattered;"[5] and to those who apprehended Him He said, "I was daily with you in the temple teaching, and ye took me not: *but the scriptures must be fulfilled*."[6]

[1] Mark xiv. 27, 28. [2] xiv. 30. [3] xiv. 22—25. [4] xiv. 21.
[5] xiv. 27. [6] xiv. 49.

Though we are nowhere told what is meant by "the gospel," yet it is evident that Jesus, to a great extent, identified it with Himself. "Whosoever," He says, "shall lose his life for my sake and the gospel's, the same shall save it."[1] "There is no man that hath left house, or brethren, or sisters, or father, or mother, or wife, or children, or lands, for my sake, and the gospel's, but he shall receive a hundredfold."[2] He distinctly declared that the gospel would be published among all nations, and that it would be preached throughout the whole world, while His last commandment to His disciples was that they should go into all the world, and preach the gospel to every creature.[3] What could be meant by this if it were not the story of the life and death of Him who had identified Himself therewith, who was Himself the sum and substance of the gospel? It is difficult to understand what the writer of this gospel

---

[1] Mark viii. 35. [2] x. 29, 30. [3] xiii. 10; xiv. 9; xvi. 15.

could have intended to convey to his readers, or what they could have derived from it, if the history of the life of Jesus was not it. We do not find any formal inculcations of doctrine, but the simple story of a life; none of the dogmas which afterwards became so conspicuous in the polemics of the Church, but specimens of the discourses and the teaching of Jesus, the record of many of His miracles and a few of His parables.

Little doubt, however, is left upon the mind as to the notion which the writer had formed of the person of Jesus, or which he manifestly intended his readers to form. The gospel was the gospel of the Son of God, who, however, prefers oftener to call Himself by the equally significant title of Son of man. He is also very clearly depicted as the Christ. On one occasion, He Himself, when asked by the high-priest, "Art thou the Christ, the Son of the Blessed?" says distinctly, "I am."[1] When Pilate asks Him, "Art thou the

[1] Mark xiv. 62.

King of the Jews?" which could have but one meaning, He answers in the accustomed and unambiguous formula, "Thou sayest."[1] It is as King of the Jews, that is to say, as the Christ, that He is crucified.[2] And, finally, the centurion, who stood over against Him, and witnessed His death, was constrained to confess, "Truly this man was the Son of God."[3] The impression left therefore on the mind by the Gospel of St. Mark,—supposing we had no other Christian document to fall back upon, or supposing we had been among those into whose hands that document had at the first accidentally fallen, being, as it must have been intended by its author to be, an adequate expression of the gospel he was recording,—is, and could have been no other than this: that the history and the knowledge of the person of Jesus was itself the gospel. He claimed to be, and was described as being, one who had power on earth

---

[1] Mark xv. 2.   [2] xv. 26.   [3] xv. 39.

to forgive sins; one whom the spiritual world obeyed; one who would be the future judge of men; one who, when He chose, could control the powers of nature and the opposition of circumstances; one who was the main subject of prophecy, and through belief in whom there was the hope of victory over death.

This was one side of His character, but on the other there was the evidence of one who was so truly human that He won sympathy to Himself by His participation in the accidents of mortality. He stood greatly in need of prayer, and was in the constant habit of seeking refuge and of finding spiritual strength in communion with God.[1] He could even become susceptible of anger and grief at the spectacle of unbelieving hardness of heart.[2] He was so much the heir of human infirmity that, after a day of continued exertion, He could fall asleep in the boat for very weariness.[3] He was

[1] Mark i. 35; vi. 46; xiv. 32—39. [2] iii. 5. [3] iv. 38.

uniformly kind and compassionate to those who came to Him in trouble and sorrow, whether as in the case of Simon's wife's mother, who was laid low with fever;[1] or the ruler of the synagogue whose little daughter was at the point of death;[2] or the woman with the issue of blood, who shrank from public observation;[3] or the man who was deaf and dumb;[4] or the little children who were brought to Him that He should touch them:[5] but to the hypocrites, and those who resisted the entrance of truth, His severity was unmitigated, whether they were those who received the fearful denunciation, "He that shall blaspheme against the Holy Ghost hath never forgiveness, but is in danger of eternal damnation: because they said, He hath an unclean spirit;"[6] or the Pharisees who laid aside the commandment of God that they might hold the tradition of men;[7] or those to whom

[1] Mark i. 31. [2] v. 23. [3] v. 27. [4] vii. 32. [5] x. 14.
[6] iii. 29, 30. [7] vii. 8.

He said there should no sign be given;[1] or those who raised the previous question of the authority on which He wrought works which they could neither deny nor blame;[2] or those who devoured widows' houses, and for a pretence made long prayers, who, He said, should receive the greater damnation.[3]

We read of His looking up to heaven and blessing the loaves when He fed the five thousand;[4] of His looking up to heaven and sighing when He healed the deaf and dumb man;[5] of His refusing the epithet 'good' which the rich man applied to Him.[6]

Though it is manifest that He had a distinct idea of the end that was coming upon Him, and, as we have seen, took particular pains to impress it upon His disciples, yet He nowhere appears to desire their condolence or seeks to move their

---

[1] Mark viii. 12.   [2] xi. 33.   [3] xii. 40.   [4] vi. 41.
[5] vii. 34.   [6] x. 18.

sympathy. He does, indeed, once remind them that they have the poor with them always, and may at any time do them good, but Him they have not alway;[1] but even in the garden, when He is constrained to say, "My soul is exceeding sorrowful, even unto death," He does not ask His disciples to pray for Him, but says, "Watch *ye* and pray, lest *ye* enter into temptation."[2] It was the agony in the garden which, in two respects, brought out the true humanity of Jesus; first, in the conflict, or at any rate the struggle, which was manifest between His own will and the Father's, when, being sore amazed and very heavy, He said three times, "Abba, Father, all things are possible unto Thee; take away this cup from me: nevertheless not what I will, but what Thou wilt;"[3] and, secondly, in the manifest accession of strength which He derived from His thrice-repeated prayer. When returning to His disciples the third time,

[1] Mark xiv. 7. [2] xiv. 34, 38. [3] xiv. 36.

He could say with calmness and resolution, "The hour is come; behold, the Son of man is betrayed into the hands of sinners. Rise up, let us go; lo, he that betrayeth me is at hand."[1] At such moments we not only feel with Him, but see also that He felt with us.

There is one other utterance which brings this out yet more plainly; it is that solemn one at the ninth hour, when He cried with a loud voice, "My God, my God, why hast Thou forsaken me?"[2] words which show that the experience of a God-forsaken man was then felt by Him whose life had been one of unbroken union with God, and which must be taken in connection with His former declarations that He came to give His life a ransom for many, and that the cup of thanksgiving was His blood of the new testament, which was shed for many, as well as with the statement of the writer himself, that the Scripture was fulfilled

[1] Mark xiv. 41, 42.   [2] xv. 34.

which saith, "And He was numbered with the transgressors."[1]

There are special features connected with the death of Jesus which are of prominent import in the record of the evangelist; for example, His being condemned as guilty of death on the ground of His claiming to be the Son of God; His having the murderer Barabbas preferred before Him; His being crucified in defiance of the governor's wish, with mock solemnity, as the King of the Jews; the darkness which overspread the whole land for the three hours from noon till He yielded up the ghost; and the fact that simultaneously with His death the veil of the temple was rent in twain from the top to the bottom. It is plain from all this that the evangelist intended to bring his readers to adopt the centurion's conclusion, "Truly this man was the Son of God."

Two more principal events complete the

[1] Mark xv. 28.

Gospel of St. Mark; the one being the burial of Jesus on the evening before the Sabbath, and the other His resurrection on the first day of the week. We are not concerned to inquire into the genuineness of the last twelve verses of the book (of their authenticity we have not the slightest doubt), the fact that the writer intended to convey the impression that Jesus had risen from the dead is indubitable, even if we stop at the eighth verse of the sixteenth chapter, for we must not forget that Jesus had distinctly promised four times that He would rise again, and had said in the Mount of Olives on the night of His passion, "After that I am risen, I will go before you into Galilee."[1] It is obvious, therefore, that the evangelist intended his readers to believe that Jesus truly died, and was buried, and rose again from the dead.

Such then, according to St. Mark, is "The

[1] Mark xiv. 28.

gospel of Jesus Christ the Son of God." It is most manifestly a gospel of fact, and of facts relating to a person. The facts recorded may have involved doctrines, but they are distinct from them. The gospel as it is presented is a gospel of incident and circumstance. It is conveyed in the Life and Death and Resurrection of the man Christ Jesus, which can only be interpreted when taken in connection with His character and teaching and claims. But the inference that we are to draw is suggested rather than enforced. We are left to form our own conclusion, but it is impossible to give to each element in the story its due weight,—the character of Jesus, the tenor and drift of His teaching, the position He assumed, the unique circumstances of His death, the definite promise He gave of His resurrection, and the way in which the promise was understood to have been redeemed,—and yet arrive at any other conclusion than one. It is only by keeping back one or more of these elements, or slurring over their importance, or shutting our eyes to their mutual relation and combined force, that we can deny the strength and justice of the writer's position. Regarded from his own standpoint his position is secure. At present we are concerned to understand what his position was rather than to estimate its justice; we want to form some definite notion of what the primitive gospel was, and we find that it consisted of the story of a person who lived and died and rose again, whose advent had been foretold by prophecy, who, having returned to heaven, should come again to judge the world, who was Himself the source of spiritual life and the Saviour of mankind. The narrative of St. Mark, from the announcement of John that He should baptise with the Holy Ghost, to the taunt of the chief priests and scribes, "He saved others, Himself He cannot save,"[1] shows this. That was the estimate which His

[1] Mark xv. 31.

forerunner on the one hand and His enemies on the other had formed of His work and office. As far as our evidence avails, and confining our inquiry for convenience' sake to one of the earliest received records, the gospel, as it was originally proclaimed and published, could not have been very different from this. As far as we know, the foundation of the edifice which we can trace in the New Testament must at least have been this or something very similar to this. The gospel of the kingdom was the message of a king, and the nucleus of the message was the story of the life and death and resurrection of the king himself. And thus the beginning of the gospel of Jesus Christ, as St. Mark shows us, must be that simple narrative of fact which brings Him before us, attracts and wins us, assures us of access, and sets us in direct relation to Him as a present and living person who is the very and eternal Son of God.

III.

THE EFFECTS OF THE PRIMITIVE GOSPEL.

THE EFFECTS OF THE PRIMITIVE GOSPEL.

Acts v. 42.

And daily in the temple, and in every house, they ceased not to teach and preach Jesus Christ.

HAVING endeavoured to ascertain, at least approximately what the primitive gospel was as it was originally preached, let us next inquire what the immediate effects were which followed from its preaching? As in the former case we were more anxious to inquire into the nature of the gospel itself than to debate the abstract question of its truth, because the ground occupied was comparatively speaking unassailable, so now the position assumed can scarcely be regarded as open to question. We have not now to defend the genuineness of the various writings preserved to us in the New Testament. We merely take those writings as existing specimens of the earliest Christian literature. Whatever else they are they undoubtedly must be that. Quite independently, therefore, of any intrinsic worth they may possess, they are manifestly certain definite and appreciable results of the early spread of Christianity—of the first preaching of the gospel. It may be difficult to determine what use St. Paul made of the mass of material which has been preserved to us in the existing gospels, or how far he was familiar with much of it, whether he was acquainted, for example, with the peculiar parabolic teaching of our Lord, and with the details of many of His miracles; but it is obvious that there was a substratum of teaching common to him and the evangelists, which he has at times briefly summarised, as for instance in the opening of his epistle to Rome, and in the fifteenth chapter of his first epistle to Corinth. Certainly the subject-matter of the four gospels, so far as it concerns Jesus Christ, is that also of St. Paul's epistles. It is the gospel of Jesus Christ which he proclaims, or rather, which his letters assume to have been proclaimed. We may imagine or discover what we please of diversity, either in those epistles themselves, or between them and the gospels, or between them and the other writings and epistles, but there is at any rate a certain unity and similarity too. Everywhere we can trace the belief in a Jesus who had been crucified and died, who had also risen again from the dead, but was nowhere to be found on earth; not seldom we find traces of a belief that this same Jesus is to return again to judgment. Everywhere we find that this new belief, which always appears as of recent date, has produced an entire revolution of thought and life wherever it has been received. St. Mark's parable of the gradual growth of seed is vividly illustrated in any one of St. Paul's epistles: "So is the kingdom of God, as if a man should cast seed into the ground; and should sleep, and rise night and day, and the seed should spring and grow up, he knoweth not how."[1] We may dispute as to what the actual seed was; but at Rome, at Corinth, at Thessalonica there is the seed grown up.

And everywhere we can discern tokens at least of what the seed must have been. The disciples at Philippi may have been ignorant of nine-tenths of the subject-matter of St. Mark's Gospel, but they are not ignorant of the other tenth. They had become "servants of Jesus Christ," and "saints in Christ Jesus," they had "fellowship in the gospel," they "looked forward to the day of Jesus Christ," they were "filled with the fruits of righteousness which are by Jesus Christ, to the glory and praise of God."[2] It was

[1] Mark iv. 26, 27.   [2] Phil. i. 1, 11.

the subject of the apostle's rejoicing in prison, that every way Christ was preached,[1] and he supposed that they could understand what that meant. For he knew that it would turn to his salvation through their prayers and the supply of the Spirit of Jesus Christ.[2] He desired "to depart and to be with Christ," but at all events he exhorted them to let their "conversation be as it became the gospel of Christ," for it was given to them "not only to believe in Christ, but also to suffer for His sake."[3] They were well aware that Jesus Christ took upon Him "the form of a servant, and was made in the likeness of men, and became obedient unto death, even the death of the Cross, wherefore," he said, "God also hath highly exalted Him, and given Him a name which is above every name: that at the name of Jesus every knee should bow, and every tongue should confess that Jesus Christ is Lord, to the glory of God the Father."[4] Com-

[1] Phil. i. 18. [2] i. 19. [3] i. 23, 27, 29. [4] ii. 7—11.

pare this, by the way, with St. Mark's narrative of the sequel to the cure of the man possessed with Legion.[1] It was "for the work of Christ" that Epaphroditus "was sick, nigh unto death."[2] It was for Christ Jesus, as they knew, that he himself "had suffered the loss of all things."[3] He desired that he might "know Christ, and the power of His resurrection, and the fellowship of His sufferings, being made conformable unto His death,"[4] and he exhorted them to be like-minded, and to walk after His example; for, said he, "our conversation is in heaven; from whence also we look for the Saviour, the Lord Jesus Christ: who shall change our vile body, that it may be fashioned like unto His glorious body, according to the working whereby He is able even to subdue all things unto Himself."[5]

Now, here it is obvious that we meet with the

[1] Mark v. 19, 20. [2] Phil. ii. 30. [3] iii. 8.
[4] iii. 10. [5] iii. 15, 20, 21.

EFFECTS OF THE PRIMITIVE GOSPEL. 97

framework of fact recorded in St. Mark's gospel, namely, the life, the death, the resurrection of the Lord Jesus, who is regarded as the Saviour, as the bestower of the Spirit, as the future Judge, as being, in short, Himself the central and substantial fact of the gospel. It is assumed, moreover, that the disciples of Christ must be partakers of His sufferings after the tenor of the words, "Whosoever will come after Me, let him deny himself, and take up his cross, and follow Me,"[1] and that the character of Christ is to be reproduced in His disciples. It is clear also that the example and influence of the life and death and resurrection of Jesus Christ have operated, precisely in the way which He indicated when He said that "new wine must be put into new bottles."[2] For the mere existence of a document like this in itself speaks volumes. It is an evidence indeed of the mind of the writer, but

[1] Mark vii. 34.   [2] ii. 22.

it is an evidence likewise of the mind of those to whom he wrote. How came there to be a society at Philippi who were capable of being written to in this way, who had recently and suddenly become ardent emulators of a spiritual standard to which they had before been strangers, and of which the world at large was ignorant? No answer can be given except one—the apostle could thank God for their "fellowship in the gospel."[1] The influence of the gospel of Jesus Christ had been brought to bear upon them, and it had made them Christians. They had obeyed the impulse which had been communicated to them by the preaching of the life and death and resurrection of Jesus Christ, and of all which that involved. It is impossible to read this short epistle and not see that it breathes an atmosphere and a spirit of which the entire literature either of Greece and Rome, not to say of

---

[1] Phil. i. 3, 5.

the whole heathen world, affords no single instance or example. That atmosphere or spirit is professedly and ostensibly the grace and spirit of Jesus Christ. It was the direct and immediate result of the preaching of His gospel. That gospel had drawn these men's hearts to Him, and in drawing them to Him it had made them what they were. This is the simple explanation of an undeniable phenomenon, and none other can be given.

Nor is it in any degree a matter for surprise that the tone and character of the Epistle to the Philippians, for example, is very different from that of the Gospel of St. Mark. It could hardly fail to be so. Even allowing that both may have been produced within a few years of one another, yet the two represent an interval of some thirty years in time, and the difference of two continents in space. One is at any rate the expression of Semitic thought, and the record of a life passed in Syria; the other was at least addressed to persons possessed of a certain amount of Greek culture, and familiar with very different thoughts and scenes than those of Palestine. The wonder rather is that there should be anything, or at least so much, in common, and that in the after development of the epistle there should be so plainly manifest the entire skeleton of the gospel. It is not too much to say, that if this framework of fact were withdrawn the very existence of the epistle would have been impossible. There would have been no motive for writing it. "Grace and peace from God the Father and the Lord Jesus Christ" would have been nonentities, and as phrases would have been unintelligible. There would have been no message of either, and no response to either, for there would have been no proof of either. Not only the substance of the letter, but its very occasion would have failed. And the same may without doubt be said of every one of St. Paul's epistles. They are a standing and imperishable witness to the gospel which he preached, to the fact that he proclaimed the life and death and resurrection, the present spirit and the future glory, of the Lord Jesus Christ.

Taking, then, the Epistle to the Philippians, for example, as a correct specimen of the belief of the Christian Church in an important town of Macedonia, at a period of some thirty years after the death of Christ, we have to bear in mind that thirty, or five and thirty, years before it was written there is nowhere any trace discoverable of anything like the gospel, whether we understand thereby its history or its teaching. It is also undeniable that the epistle represents a further development of the stage of thought indicated by the gospel. Whatever may be their respective dates as compositions, there can be no doubt that the epistle represents an advancement on the thought of the gospel, just as the writings of Augustine or Luther represent an advancement on the thought of St. Paul's epistles. The gospel of St. Mark, for example, could not have been developed from the slender basis of fact discernible in the letter to Philippi, though it is conceivable that the facts in the letter to Philippi might have been condensed from those recorded in the gospel.

It is impossible, therefore, to suppose that the story of the gospel as it appears, for example, in the Epistle to the Philippians can have originated as a myth in the thirty or five and thirty years, that is to say, in the single generation before that epistle was written, especially when we bear in mind the character of those years. And yet within that time we have conclusive proof that it must have originated. But if it did not originate as a myth it must either have originated as a true story or as the falsified and exaggerated version of a true story. Now, whatever there may be in the Gospel of St. Mark, there is no evidence of exaggeration in the story as it appears in the letter to Philippi. The most prominent, or at least the central, feature in the story of Christ as it there appears is His death. But it is precisely the death of Christ which is that feature least likely or possible to have been exaggerated or invented. The evidence for the death of Christ is only to be characterised as overwhelming. Whatever difficulties, scientific or otherwise, may surround the fact of His resurrection, of His true and actual death, however occasioned, there can be no reasonable doubt, nor that it was accomplished on the cross. It is simply monstrous to pretend to affirm that the story of the crucifixion of Jesus was the result of mythical exaggeration or of invention. It is, indeed, the death of Christ so clearly foretold by Himself, and so amply testified and confirmed in a variety of independent ways, that sets the seal to His character and claims. We cannot dispute the simple fact of His death, and holding the fact of His death as it is recorded, we not only have an adequate explanation of His career and teaching, but likewise a firm and secure basis on which to rest the cumulative evidence for His resurrection.

Now, every one of the Pauline epistles—unless indeed we except the second epistle to Thessalonica and the epistle to Philemon, in which the evidence is only indirect—being written as they are to at least nine different centres of thought, extending from Galatia to Rome, bears direct and independent testimony to the fact that throughout this district of not less than twenty degrees of longitude, the death of Jesus on the cross was universally believed by those to whom the author wrote. Is it conceivable that all these people, numbering probably many thousands, should have been brought in so short a time, and, considering what it involved, to believe in a story which was virtually without foundation? What was there in the story of Christ's death specially calculated to strike the imagination, or to work upon the feelings of so many people, so various in their national peculiarities and so differently constituted? Had they all been alike deceived? were they all the victims of delusion? Had they all been duped into believing a cunningly-devised fable, or, in simple English, a lie? The notion is manifestly inconceivable. Why, barely more than thirty years had elapsed since the event believed had happened. What was there in this man's death, taken alone, to produce an impression so deep, so uniform, and so exceptional, more than in the death of Cæsar, or of Cicero, or of any one else? And is not death the appointed lot of every one? What is there remarkable, then, in the death of this man, that it should become a special topic to be dwelt upon and believed in this way, unless, being as it was a true death, it stood altogether alone and unique in the history of the world? He did indeed die—who can dispute that?—for all have died. But it was because there was no other death like His that it became the subject of belief. Nor is it possible that the notion about the death can have originated the belief in the death itself, because had the death as a fact not occurred, there would have been no foundation for the ideas concerning it, and nothing to support them. Why should the death of Christ be fixed upon as, of all others, the one remedial and atoning death, unless indeed there had been in that death, as well as in the life of Jesus, features of a totally exceptional and unique character? Nor is it possible to imagine that the general character of the life and death of Jesus was sufficient to suggest to a few more ardent and susceptible of His disciples the notion of His dying as a sacrifice for the sins of the world, and yet not sufficient to sustain it when originated, because then we should have lacked not only the evidence we have of the wide-spread extent to which it was believed, but the literary monuments which we possess could never have existed. The second half of the writings of the New Testament are themselves a witness, not only to the influence of the gospel story, but to the reality of that effect upon the nature of man which it claimed to produce. We cannot, for example, call in question or deny the high spiritual character and tone of the epistle to the Romans or Philippians without approaching very nearly to the sin of those who said of Jesus that He had an unclean spirit. They are verily an undeniable proof of what this belief in Jesus had done for one man. And seeing that they afford some evidence also of the spiritual character of those to whom they were written, they are proof likewise of what that belief had done for them. In fact, the effects of the primitive gospel, as it was first preached, of which we have ample and conclusive evidence, are themselves a proof of its origin. That which could operate as the gospel operated must either be the lie of the devil or else it must stand for ever as the truth of God. The abiding witness which He was pleased to vouchsafe to a sinful and unbelieving world of the truth and mission of His Son was written in the evidence we have of the effects which followed from the preaching of the Cross.

And it is as well to observe that in point of evidence everything turns upon the death of Christ. Of that death we may be sure, without any reasonable cause for, not to say possibility of, doubt. The early sect of the Docetæ who denied it, did so for very obvious reasons, which need not and cannot affect us now. But having got as a sure corner-stone the fact of Christ's death upon the cross, and the place it clearly occupied in early preaching, and the extent to which it was believed, we find that its very belief compels us to accept it, not only as a bare fact, but as a fact of no ordinary kind. If Jesus died thus, He must have died unjustly, and under circumstances of special injustice. But He was always called the Christ, and there is reason to believe He died professing Himself to be the Christ, and because He called Himself the Christ. But if He died professing Himself to be the Christ, and was not the Christ, He died justly. It is impossible to believe that He died unjustly, and yet had not such a character at least as would be consistent with His claim to be the Christ, or would be adequate to create or to sustain the belief, which subsequently arose, that He was the Christ. His life, therefore, must have been one of sufficient purity to warrant the belief that, dying the ignominious death He died, He was nevertheless the Christ. His death, therefore, coupled with the way in which that death was regarded, is to no small extent a voucher for the general character of His life. It is impossible that His death should have been believed in as it was, if His life had not been such as to make it appear that He died unjustly. Other men have been able to gather followers around them till death became the signal for their dispersion; but this man's death was the very signal and the motive power which drew all men unto Him. His death, therefore, must have been the seal of a correspondent life. But, in point of fact, it is the moral character of the life of Jesus which has been least assailed, for the very reason that it is unassailable. We are consequently warranted in viewing not only the life of Jesus in the light of His death, but also the death of Jesus in the light of His life. And then it becomes impossible to reject the evidence we have of the actual claims which were advanced by Jesus. Beyond all question He taught His disciples to believe that He was the Messiah. Beyond all question He was understood by His own nation to claim to be that exalted and mysterious personage. Beyond all question this claim it was that constituted the indictment upon which He suffered. We are shut up, therefore, to the conclusion either that Jesus, being what He professed to be, was willing to die for the profession, or else that, not being what He professed to be, He was, as His enemies alleged, a deceiver, blasphemous and profane, who was worthy to die because guilty of high treason against the Majesty of Heaven, in which case, what becomes of His moral character, which we are constrained to acknowledge as unsullied ?

And, brethren, taking all the facts into consideration, and honestly facing them, there is no middle position. If we find it reasonable, upon the evidence, to decide that Jesus was a deceiver who was guilty of the most outrageous blasphemy, then by all means be it so, let us like truth-loving honest men, as we profess to be, come to that decision and accept it; but if, on the other hand, from the evidence we find it impossible to do so, then there is no middle position, we must, like brave and suffering men, accept the one alternative, whatever it may cost us. The life of Jesus was a life of unimpeachable and spotless purity. The claims He consistently advanced were an intrinsic and integral element of that life; and the death of infamy on the cross was the seal and consummation of the life, the consequence and attestation of the claims which were advanced.

And having thus arrived at what is virtually, and must ever remain, an impregnable position, resting upon solid historical evidence, deep and broad, altogether independent of a variety of minor questions which may be mooted around but cannot touch it, every step of our subsequent career becomes, comparatively speaking, easy. The evidence for the resurrection of Christ virtually resolves itself into the evidence for His death and for His life. If He truly lived as He lived, and died as He died, and we believe it, then the belief in His resurrection follows, not indeed as a matter of course, but as the fitting and necessary part of a consistent whole. It is difficult to reject the evidence, clear and explicit as we have seen it to be, that Jesus told His disciples He would rise again; and if so, the fact of His resurrection, like that of His Messiahship, must stand or fall with the integrity of His moral character and the circumstances and reality of His death. We are not called upon first to prove the resurrection of Christ and then decide upon His claims, but to decide upon His claims and to estimate the bearing of his death upon His claims, and of His claims upon His death, and then to weigh the evidence for the resurrection, not independently of, or apart from, but in consideration of the antecedent probability for it thereby created.

And, taking the several points in this order, it is possible that we may come to the conclusion at which Peter arrived, that "God raised Him up, having loosed the pains of death, because it was not possible that He should be holden of it." But however this may be, certain it is that the whole strength of each evangelist is so to say concentrated upon the death of Jesus, not upon His resurrection. It is the death which is the central feature of the story. It is that momentous fact which we are invited to behold in its length and breadth, as we are to-day,[1] and when we have taken that in, but not before, we shall be in a position to estimate the evidence for the resurrection. It is the fashion to speak of that evidence as it is furnished in the gospels as unsatisfactory,

[1] Preached upon Good Friday, April 3, 1874.

inconclusive, and contradictory. I believe, when rightly estimated, it is as full and ample as we can desire: into that matter it is not now proposed to enter; but we must never forget that the resurrection stands not alone, but together and in immediate and inseparable connection with the death and the life and the teaching of Jesus.

It must, however, at all events be admitted that the fact of the resurrection was a prominent feature in the early testimony concerning Jesus. Whatever may be the verdict which we pass upon the authenticity of the Acts, that book constitutes at least the only source from whence we can derive any notion of the events which immediately followed the close of the gospel history. Nor is there any reason to believe that the statement in the text will be controverted by any one. Beyond all question, this is how the first disciples acted in Jerusalem in the early days of the Church. Daily in the temple, and in every house, they ceased not to teach and preach Jesus Christ. May we not fairly ask, What could possess them to do so? If the statement is one of fact, as there is no reason to doubt, then the fact is at least as marvellous and unaccountable as any of the apparently miraculous incidents recorded in the narrative. We may well be content to leave them alone while we have so ordinary and commonplace, and yet withal so strange and unaccountable a circumstance to deal with as this. A few months, apparently, after the death of Jesus, the very men who had fled from Him at His apprehension are still found at Jerusalem, seizing every opportunity of proclaiming His name and story. They are not the heralds of any particular theory or doctrine, for they are one and all illiterate men, but they are simple witnesses to a fact. Their language was, " We cannot but speak the things which we have seen and heard." They bore testimony to those things of which they were assured on the evidence of their senses. They had seen many times, they had conversed, they had eaten and drunk with the very man Jesus, who had been put to death for calling Himself the Christ. And they persisted now, in a way they never had before, in declaring Him to be the Christ. It was equally useless to put them in prison, or to beat them, or to charge them to hold their peace. They departed from the presence of the council rejoicing that they were counted worthy to suffer shame for His name. Such dogged and unaccountable obstinacy had never been witnessed before, and moreover it was altogether unlike anything they had themselves previously manifested. A great change had passed over them, which seemed to have remoulded their natural character, and all that their adversaries could do was to take knowledge of them that they had been with Jesus.

It is, moreover, certain that a very prominent feature of their teaching was the resurrection of

Jesus. There, in the very place where He had been crucified, where during His life He appears to have been very well known, where all the circumstances of His death must have been perfectly familiar, the precautions that were taken about His burial, and the strange rumours that were in circulation afterwards—there these illiterate men were coming into collision with the legal authorities and ecclesiastical magnates of the day, because the persuasion was maintained by, and could not be beaten out of, them that their Master, who was crucified, had risen from the dead. The story was on the face of it so obviously absurd that we are at a loss whether to be more astonished at the pertinacity of the disciples or at the anxiety of their opponents to quash their testimony. One would have thought that the story, from its very nature, was one that might safely be left to die a natural death. This, however, it appeared to have no tendency to do; but, on the contrary, we read that "believers were the more added unto the Lord, multitudes both of men and women;"[1] that "the number of the disciples multiplied in Jerusalem greatly; and that a great company of the priests were obedient to the faith."[2] And it is perfectly certain that this "faith" can have been none other than faith in the resurrection of Jesus, or that at any rate it must have included that belief, because the fact of the death of Jesus was just at that time too notorious to be a matter merely of belief. It was accepted as a certainty, and no one thought of doubting it; but it was not properly speaking a matter of faith, any more than our knowledge of the death of Napoleon the Third, or of any other recent and notorious event, could be called a matter of faith. If, then, people believed in Jesus at all, they must have believed either in His being the Christ or in His having risen from the dead: as a matter of fact they

[1] Acts v. 14.   [2] vi. 7.

believed both; of that there is abundant evidence and no possible room for doubt.

And, indeed, why should the very people who had slain Him be found among the first to acknowledge Him as the Christ, unless after His death something had occurred of so important a nature as to lead them totally to reverse their decision about Him. What that something had been we are at a loss to conjecture, but we may well doubt whether the mere *groundless* belief in His resurrection, capable as the story then was of immediate and conclusive refutation and disproof if untrue, would have been able to operate in the same way. Unquestionably, mere compunction for the death of Jesus, because it had been inflicted undeservedly, would have been inadequate to work so complete a revulsion of feeling, and produce such results (both of which are undeniable), just as in the present day the sudden discovery, upon subsequent evidence, that a criminal had been executed unjustly would be inadequate to excite any other feelings than those of intense popular indignation and regret, which, however, would soon spend themselves and be forgotten.

But here it was manifestly quite otherwise. No mere compunctions about the death of Jesus would have sufficed to change a man's convictions about His being the Christ (more especially as in many cases there can have been no room, properly speaking, for any compunction at all: those who believed had not all of them consented unto His death), however such a change of conviction about His being the Christ, in whatever way produced, would necessarily have involved an entire change of opinion about His death. Thus, again, it appears that the death of Jesus is virtually the corner-stone of the evidence for His resurrection. Till we have determined what was the nature and bearing of that death we are not really in a position to estimate fairly the evidence for His resurrection. It would be perfectly absurd to suppose that all, or a tenth part, or even a hundredth part of the early believers in the resurrection of Jesus had judicially investigated that evidence, or were capable of doing so. The evidence which carried conviction home to their minds then, was the way in which the belief in that resurrection was still spreading itself, and was operating wherever it spread. They themselves felt the power of it as they had never felt any influence before; and when they surrendered themselves to it, they found it not only irresistible, but salutary and regenerating in its effects. They did under the influence of it what others could not do—they could forego personal advantage, and could love one another. Of this there remains to the present day overwhelming and irrefragable evidence.

EFFECTS OF THE PRIMITIVE GOSPEL. 123

It was in this way that the earliest belief in the resurrection was found to operate. They who accepted it could do what before was inconceivable, and wholly unintelligible,—they could spend their days in teaching and preaching Jesus Christ. Their testimony may or may not have been accompanied with what our scientific education would recognise as miracles,—that is a question we are content now to waive,—but here, in what they did, in their life and conduct and changed occupations and altered feelings and extraordinary success, was the greatest miracle of all. They were not only a sign unto all the world, but they were a sign unto themselves, and not only a sign unto themselves, but a sign unto all the world. There was a new life working in them, they could not help feeling it, others could not help seeing it, and it was a life derived from and communicated by a person who had been dead. The life came from Jesus Christ, was centred in Jesus Christ, followed the preaching of Jesus Christ, and was limited to the area of that preaching. The very mention of His name wrought wonders. He seemed to be present as a distinct personal influence and agency wherever those who believed in Him were met together. What other dead man's influence or memory has ever acted in a manner similar or analogous to this? Setting aside every miraculous feature in the Acts of the Apostles as unworthy of credit or what not, the mere production of the book itself, with its unimpeachable testimony to the early spread of the gospel, and the mere existence of the Pauline epistles, exaggerate the apparent discrepancies between them and the Acts as we may, to say nothing of the existence of other early Christian literature and known Christian conduct, is a witness to the discovery of a new and original power working in many and varied centres of life, which cannot on any known or natural principles be ascribed to the moral influence of the *death* only of a person, however exalted his character or dear his memory. We must postulate some other invisible cause, and there is no known cause but one.

The position, then, at which we arrive, and appear to be warranted in arriving, is this: The death of Jesus may safely be assumed as an historic fact. The effects also which immediately followed that death are certain, as attested by the Acts of the Apostles, the writings of St. Paul, early Christian literature, and the known condition of Christianity from the first. These effects are undeniable, whatever opinion we may hold as to the composition or authenticity of the Acts, or the genuineness of many of the Pauline writings. These writings, whether we regard them as merely human, or in a sense Divine, afford testimony which is incontrovertible to the prevalence of a belief, and the nature of it. There were numbers, both in Greece and Rome, within the first generation after the death of Christ, whose life and character had been entirely remodelled and reconstituted by their belief in Him. The effects produced by this belief are at once obvious and permanent. We cannot shut our eyes to them. But they cannot be accounted for by that death alone.

The mere recollection or influence of one departed would have been totally inadequate to produce them. He may have died never so unjustly, but the belief that He so died would have been inoperative at Rome, and insufficient to produce the effects which we know were produced there. We cannot discover anything even in the circumstances of Christ's death, taken alone, which was calculated to work as we find the knowledge of His death working. We are compelled, therefore, to postulate another element as the cause of an effect so striking. And, associated with the knowledge of the death of Christ, as a fact we find the *belief* that He was the Christ, and that He had risen from the dead. This belief, also, as being very general and widespread, admits of no doubt. The result of it was the rise of an entirely new and original literature, to which there is no parallel in the history of the world, certainly not of the heathen world. The Epistle to the Romans, as an existing literary monument, is at least a phenomenon to which the literature of Greece and Rome affords no parallel, whether we regard the sentiments of the writer, or still more, the state of feeling to which it appeals. The Acts of the Apostles, even if it were from first to last a romance, and no matter whether it was written within the first century or not, is a witness to the existence of a public to whom it would be acceptable, who could take an interest in, and were capable of being edified by, such unusual, such unnatural, and such dry details as those of itinerant preachers declaring the necessity of repentance and conversion from idol-worship, and of faith in one Jesus, who was dead, who was affirmed by some then to be alive. There was clearly, therefore, in existence a society which was anxious to be informed as to its early history, and whether this history was authentic or not, it was at any rate the only one presentable. But the mere existence of such a society, which was very widespread within thirty years after its supposed origin, whether this was its history or not, was itself a phenomenon. And we have abundant evidence of the general character, aims, and standard of the people calling themselves Christians, of the way in which their absurd and extraordinary belief worked. Whether or not the earliest portrait of them, as having all things common, of parting with their lands and houses for the poor, and the like, was overdrawn or not, it is clear that such a portrait was admired; that as it was wholly original, so also it was not without its practical fruits. It is certain that many, like the apostles, devoted themselves to teaching and preaching Jesus Christ; that many, like Paul and Barnabas, travelled about doing so; and the history of their travels, being entirely devoid of the kind of interest which we should appreciate in such works, was found attractive to many, and only because of the belief it fostered, the spirit inculcated, and the examples recorded.

Now let us bear in mind that in the face of all these facts we must either say they were accounted for by the sentiments aroused by the proclamation of the death of Jesus alone, or that they were caused by the additional element of belief in His resurrection. We are secure in saying that they could not have been caused without that *belief*, because there is abundant evidence of its being the principal motive influence. The only question, therefore, that can arise is this,

Would such results as these have been produced by the belief in the resurrection of Jesus, if it had been belief only—that is to say, belief without foundation in fact? And in answer to this question, we are bold to affirm, that belief in His resurrection, if it had been a fiction, could not have produced the results which we know were produced by it, which we can see for ourselves did follow it.

In other words, the earliest results of the first preaching of the gospel, the way in which it was preached, and the effects which followed its preaching, as they are attested in the writings of St. Paul and in those portions of the Acts of the Apostles which, being devoid of miraculous details, are not, as substantially authentic history, open to question,—are themselves the greatest evidence of its origin. That which could work and did work as this primitive gospel of the life, death, and resurrection of Jesus Christ worked, must have been Divine. No other power but the power of God could produce such results. For they were not natural, but contrary to nature, thwarting the inclinations and tendencies of the natural heart. Infatuation alone would have spent itself and died away. The mere sentiment occasioned by the death of Christ would have been inoperative. Belief in the resurrection of Jesus, if, as a matter of fact, His body had been mouldering in the tomb, would have failed to act as this belief acted, like an arrow that falls far short of the mark. Everywhere there is the evidence of the operation of a present person, who is invisible but all-powerful, whose special sphere of influence is the heart. It is the power of the presence of Jesus Christ, who is no longer dead, but is alive. We may leave the sensible evidence for the resurrection, satisfactory as it really is, to take care of and adjust itself, if we honestly and sincerely give to this spiritual and abiding evidence its due weight. It is only by depreciating the results actually produced, disregarding their true character, assigning to them false motives, under-estimating their magnitude and their purity, that we can deprive it of its power. There are the indications of an influence at work which is new in the history of the world, and the effects which follow it are new. Wherever it comes it begets new life; it casts out the old and brings in the new. The old impulses and old aims, the old hopes and old fears are forgotten, and give place to others never experienced before. New desires, new motives, new objects are felt and pursued. The occupations and the character are changed, and life itself is regenerated and renewed in its hidden springs.

Judge for yourselves, my brethren, of the evidence which the earliest Christian writings afford of this. Measure the difference between the life of a man who can say, "To me to live is Christ, and to die is gain,"[1] and that of one who is destitute of the Christian's hope, and then say whether this is the evidence of the spiritual operation of a person who has triumphed over death, or of one who has himself succumbed to it.

[1] Phil. i. 2.

IV.

THE REGENERATIVE POWER OF THE GOSPEL.

THE REGENERATIVE POWER OF THE GOSPEL.

Revelation xxi. 5.

And He that sat upon the throne said, Behold, I make all things new, and He said unto me, Write: for these words are true and faithful.

The evidence we possess of the manner in which the first preaching of the gospel worked is so complete and satisfactory as to be irresistible when fairly considered. That evidence may be briefly described in one word as the creation of an entirely new literature. It matters, comparatively speaking, little how we regard that literature or account for its origin; whether we prefer to dwell upon the obviously human accidents and causes by which it was produced, or upon the sufficiently patent indications it presents of an origin other than human,—a controlling and inspiring agency which was Divine; regarded merely as a literature which, like every other literature, reflects the character of the people among whom it arose, it is in itself the evidence of a motive power and influence at work which was new in the history of the world.

The four gospels, apart from the question who may have written them, the Acts of the Apostles, the letters ascribed to St. Paul, whether all these various works fall within the first century or not, are at least the monuments of an energy put forth which has never been repeated since. That energy may be characterised as an intense belief in the person of Jesus Christ, a loving memory and trust in the power of His death, a faith in His resurrection. It is certain that no one of these elements can be left out, least of all the belief in His resurrection. The Christian literature not only bears evidences of the strength of this belief in those by whom it was written, but, we may safely say, could not have been produced without it. We have got, then, as an indispensable element in the production of the Christian literature, and in the effects of the early preaching of the gospel, a strong faith in the resurrection of the Lord Jesus. It cannot be denied that this was the backbone of the creed of the early Church. Neither can it be doubted that in the strength of this faith extraordinary results were brought about, such as had never before been witnessed among men. The picture drawn, for example, by the Apostle Paul, in his second letter to Corinth, of the labours of himself and his colleagues, gives us some idea of the nature of those results, leaving out altogether any others which may be regarded as supernatural. These labours were undertaken not for the acquisition of wealth or for the sake of fame, or pleasure, or personal advantage of any kind, but solely to make known what he called the unsearchable riches of Christ. And it is not too much to say, that the very conception of such an idea or of such a motive was entirely new. We are constrained, therefore, to ask whether, seeing that particular results were brought about by faith in the resurrection of Jesus Christ, it is possible to believe that the same results would have followed if that faith had rested upon no foundation? Because it must be borne in mind, that either Jesus Christ did rise from the dead or He did not: there is no middle alternative. If His disciples and the first preachers were merely deluded and deceived into the persuasion that He rose from the dead, then He simply did not rise, and we have to account for the actual phenomena presented in the literature and in the known conduct of the first believers on the hypothesis that belief in the resurrection was based on a mistake. But it is surely no extravagant position to maintain that the way in which belief in the resurrection worked during the first half century after its origin affords very significant indication that it was not based on a mistake. Leave out the actual fact of the resurrection, and it is hard indeed, not to say absolutely impossible, not only to account for the prevalence of the belief in it, but also for the various results which the belief produced.

The resurrection of Jesus Christ was the revelation of the source of a new life. The various writings of the New Testament are the literary monuments which attest the operation of this new life, and are the witness to its power, and as long as the world lasts they will continue to be this. The questions as to authorship and the genuineness of particular books, interesting and important as they are, may nevertheless be pronounced subordinate both in interest and importance to the palpable fact of the unique existence of the New Testament. For example, the authorship of the Epistle to the Ephesians, or of the First Epistle of St. Peter, sinks after all into comparative insignificance when contrasted with the inherent value and the intrinsic character of those writings. Even supposing that the Epistle to the Ephesians was a forgery, the sublime moral teaching of that letter would still remain, damaged undoubtedly in the weight of its influence by the recollection that he who could so teach and exhort had nevertheless a lie in his right hand; but while the human conscience remains capable of apprehending the highest moral standard, it must acknowledge that such a standard is there approached. On the very lowest supposition, therefore, the document is entitled to the position it is qualified to hold on the simple merit of its teaching. Even if a forgery, it would still serve as a specimen of the moral elevation that had been attained by the Christian Church. At best some obscure member of that Church had sought, by unwarrantable means, to gain what appeared to him to be a desirable end. It is hardly possible, on the wildest supposition, to go farther than this; and even when we go so far, though we have indeed exchanged what is genuine for what is counterfeit, yet even the counterfeit is not without a certain value of its own, for it forms an integral portion of a particular literature, which must after all stand or fall on its own merits, and not upon the merits, real or imaginary, of its supposed authors.

In like manner, if we possess in the first Epistle of St. Peter a genuine work of that apostle, its value is undoubtedly enhanced to a high degree; but if otherwise, even then it is not altogether worthless as a monument of early Christian literature, or as a witness to the teaching that was fostered and produced by the early

Christian body. The personal disadvantage attaching to the presumed forger must necessarily be deducted, but this redounds mainly upon himself unless it can be shown, which it cannot, that the body as a whole knowingly acquiesced in the imposture. And, even then, we should be confronted with the anomalous spectacle of a body of men, possessing an enlightened Christian conscience, and yet actuated by unworthy motives, which conditions, however it may be with individuals, with societies have certainly a tendency to neutralise each other—that is to say, they do not readily co-exist.

In short, the supposed case, at the worst, resembles that of a minister of the gospel possessed of great personal influence and universally respected, whose teaching is acknowledged to come with power to many and to be fruitful in its beneficent results, but whose integrity or moral character, after a long career of usefulness, is suddenly found to collapse. We have all had personal experience of such cases, and well know the shock they occasion and the disastrous influence they exert on many minds; but it is those only who have no fixed principles of their own, and no foundation in themselves, that are really injured by them. The personal influence of the teacher is for ever gone, but the value of the moral teaching, so far as it was in itself healthy and sound, is not diminished. Such characters may still shine as beacon lights to warn the traveller of the precipice, though they have ceased for ever to be guides themselves along the path of life. The power of the truth is weakened among those who have not obeyed it; but with those who have sincerely accepted it, there is added thereto a yet higher degree of solemnity by the very defection of him who was once its minister. While the Psalms of David remain for ever the priceless heritage of the faithful, it is the enemies of the Lord, and those alone, to whom he gave and continues to give, by his grievous fall, great occasion to blaspheme.

Supposing therefore that the authorship of certain books was as dubious as some would have us believe, yet even then the intrinsic value of the teaching those books inculcate would not be lessened; it would still possess an independent value which could be used as an indication of the moral standard attained by the early Church. It would serve as a proof of the kind of influence which was at work, and of the way in which it worked; and this was at once original, unexampled, and salutary.

When, however, on the other hand, we find that, in the great majority of cases, these doubts are absolutely groundless, it is obvious that the intrinsic character of the writings themselves serves to create a presumption in favour of their being the genuine works of the authors whose names they bear.[1] It is *primâ facie* more likely that productions of such a stamp should be genuine than that they should be forgeries. Their actual character must of course be determined on other and critical grounds, but until it can be shown conclusively that they must on those grounds be rejected, we are fairly entitled to the presumption which is most in accordance with their obvious internal character.

But whatever opinion we may form on this matter, it is undeniable that the New Testament, as a whole, stands alone and unrivalled in the literature of the world for the purity and elevation of its moral teaching, and the sublimity of the character it portrays to us. Here, then, is the phenomenon of an absolutely unique literature called into existence by the spontaneous operation of faith in a particular person, who lived and

---

[1] This of course does not apply to those books which are really anonymous, *e.g.* the Four Gospels, etc.

died and rose again. Faith in His life alone would not have produced it; faith in His death alone would not have produced it; the most potent element was faith in His resurrection, of the influence of which there are distinct traces in each separate document. In this we discover the new motive power which was adequate to producing the totally new results. The statement of Him that sat on the throne in the last book of the inspired collection, " Behold, I make all things new," is literally and accurately true with regard to the literature which faith in His name had called into existence; and it is when we give due consideration to the significance of this fact, that we are able to appreciate the truth of the command in its bearing on the literature at large, "Write: for these words are true and faithful." The new life, with which the writings are everywhere instinct, is an evidence of the new life which had been communicated to the writers.

They were manifestly living in the strength of a regenerated nature, which showed itself in what they wrote as well as in their actions. The world could see, and could not help seeing, that they were new men. Could such living monuments have been created by one who was not alive? Could such phenomena have been produced by a mere faith, however strong, which rested on no foundation in fact? Because, if the Lord had not risen, the faith of those men did rest on no foundation in fact. And then, in that case, we should have had an effect which was, real and palpable produced by a cause which was hollow and unreal. The new life which was so conspicuous, and was accompanied by results so new, would have been virtually an effect without a cause, seeing that any other cause than the one alleged must have involved a falsehood. And thus there would have been an essential incongruity between the nature of the cause producing, and the nature of the effect produced. There would not have been that relation in kind which must ever subsist between events that are bound together by necessary sequence. Given the resurrection of Jesus Christ, and the events which followed it are conceivable because they are analogous; take away that resurrection, and they become inexplicable and anomalous. For in the one case life produces life, and in the other it is produced by death. The phenomena which are so marvellous in themselves are intelligible on the supposition of a new impulse communicated to humanity, they are unintelligible and impossible if that impulse is withdrawn.

And thus the argument of St. Paul, which is self-evident as he puts it, "If Christ be not risen, then is our preaching vain, and your faith is also vain,"[1] is perfectly sound when put conversely: "If the preaching and the faith are not vain, then

[1] 1 Cor. xv. 14.

Christ is risen;" but we have manifest and conclusive proof that the preaching and the faith, as judged by their results, were not vain—were not vanities, but realities, and substantial realities, compared with which nothing else was so real: the natural inference, therefore, is that Christ was risen.

And this must ever remain the greatest moral evidence of the truth of the gospel. Where this evidence fails and is not appreciated, no other can succeed. It is confessedly impossible to present an argument which shall show to scientific demonstration that the gospel is the truth of God; for if otherwise, we should perforce be Christians, and the gospel would cease to be the moral touchstone of humanity. We can rise step by step from a variety of considerations to a degree of moral conviction; we can point to the natural inference as being one and no other; but the final process of the mind, by which the gospel is accepted as the truth, must be one of faith, and not of reason. We can show, by the application of scientific methods, the very high probability of its truth, but not by pure science that it is absolutely true. It is possible to show by fair argument that certain results could not have taken place but for a particular cause, but no amount of argument can suffice to remove the *a priori* objection, that that alleged cause is itself contrary to reason, and in the nature of things impossible. If any man chooses to maintain that ground, in itself perfectly intelligible and strictly logical, it is obvious that he is beyond the reach of any arguments that are simply moral. The spheres of mental operation are distinct, and they have no connecting link. It is like a struggle between the inhabitants of two worlds, neither of which can reach the other. The fact of the resurrection does not appeal to physical certainty, but to moral conviction. If a man demands physical certainty as a condition of moral conviction, it is plain that we cannot give it him, and he must abide in unbelief. That the first witnesses of the resurrection had such physical certainty is another matter, which is the subject of testimony; the testimony may be adequate, but it is manifest that physical certainty is a kind of evidence that could not be indefinitely multiplied, while its efficacy would be only co-extensive with its limits.

While, however, the facts of the gospel are not the subjects of scientific demonstration any more than other historical facts, the moral truths, of which those facts were themselves the original and the mighty impulse, are possessed of an inherent and abiding evidence. There is a tendency in the religion of the gospel which is manifest in no other religion,—always to regenerate itself. Whatever is submitted to human apprehension and human guardianship must be liable to the accidents of humanity; such as loss, deterioration, and decay. And the history of the progress of the gospel among men has sufficiently illustrated this fact. The purity, the brightness, the simplicity, the clearness of the gospel has continually been sullied and obscured by the treatment it has met with in the world. The descent, for example, from the apostolical epistles to what are know as the writings of the apostolical fathers is steep and sudden, not, however now in moral declension, so much as in intellectual power and enlightenment. Whatever vigour Christian literature may subsequently have regained, there can be no question as to the marked contrast between its first two stages. The difference between St. Paul and Ignatius, or St. John and Clement of Rome, is only too conspicuous; and it is by the very strength of this contrast that we are the better enabled to estimate the force and magnitude of that impulse which could at once and without any warning have originated such a literature as that contained in the New Testament. It can only be characterised as gigantic, as superhuman, as Divine.

But if the first effects of that impulse rapidly grew feeble, they were not exhausted. The sphere of their earliest manifestations was indeed unique; but they were destined again and again to revive and to reappear in various forms. And the book which was the first permanent expression of the new life, became itself the originating cause of a literature which is already practically infinite, and to which in the future we can assign no conceivable limits.

The earnest, indeed, of the prolific literary power which was to be exerted by the New Testament was given in the complex character of the book itself. Taking the historic gospels as, if not the earliest, at least the record of the earliest, manifestation of the gospel, the step between them and the epistles was immense. What could be more original and striking than the development therein exhibited? And yet, as being the spontaneous production of the development of natural circumstances, what could be more natural? The gospel as a gospel of fact, communicating a fresh impulse to humanity, could operate only as we see it operating in the latter half of the New Testament. How would such an energy, if communicated, express itself? Would it not be by the utterance of those sentiments of love, adoration, gratitude, and devotion that the epistles express? What more natural than for persons who had felt the same impulse to speak from the platform of their feelings, and under the circumstances to do so in the form of letters? And yet when regarded in the results the step from the simple historic record to the elaborate hortatory exposition was immense. If the gospels contain the record of the facts, the epistles contain the earliest written expression of the way in which the knowledge and the experimental reception of the facts worked.

But the literary advance was great and original. For the gospels, whatever their date, represented the recollection of a past condition of things. They were an attempt to recall the past. But the epistles were the necessary expression of the present. And inasmuch as they rested on the basis of the same facts, they can only be regarded as illustrating the results and influence of the facts. Any subsequent development of Christian literature, whether it be that of Augustine, of Luther, or of the great English theologians of the seventeenth century, is but small when compared with the gigantic but wholly natural development which is marked by the progress from the historic to the epistolary compositions of the New Testament. Therein was manifested the highest evidence of the recreative energy of the gospel.

And if literature bears witness to this, does

not history do the same? Within three centuries after the death of Christ, how vast the change which had passed over the face of the civilised world. For evil or for good (and surely few who would call themselves philosophers would say for evil) the gospel has made its way among mankind. Before very long, indeed, its light was destined to be well-nigh quenched, but still, whatever light there was, was light kindled by the gospel. It still bore its witness before men, and that witness was itself. Missionary enterprise, bright deeds of self-denial, enduring monuments of individual piety, characterise even the darkest period of the Church; and the truth is continually being exemplified that a vital principle has been communicated to mankind that can never be wholly extinguished, and is always capable of regenerating itself when human depravity has corrupted or obscured it. Even to those who reject the gospel, it is a light-bearing influence which confronts and enlightens them. They borrow light from it, to be used, indeed, oftentimes against itself. They imbibe its truth-loving principle, though for the purpose of proving it untrue. They are ready to appeal to its maxims of righteousness, integrity, and purity, to the disadvantage and condemnation of its professed adherents. Can anything display more evidently the intrinsic power of the gospel? It has provided men with a weapon of keen and heavenly temperament, which can be wielded to its own injury.

There is only one consolation in this fact, but it is a sufficient one, that all such attempts must ultimately recoil on those who make them, and redound to the glory and advantage of the gospel. Amid considerable apparent enmity there may indeed be not a little of that spirit which is not far from the kingdom of God, which, if certain impediments, constitutional, accidental, intellectual, or spiritual, were removed, would thankfully surrender itself a willing vassal of the kingdom. We must not be impatient, we must not get soon angry, and above all, we must ever remember that the cause is not ours, but God's. It cannot ultimately fail. It is not given to any of us to see more than a small portion of the truth, and that which we see is not the whole. It may be that our portion is not just now the most essential, and in being over-valiant for that we may be instrumental in retarding the progress of some other.

If the gospel is its own witness, it is also its own keeper, for it is secure in the abiding promise of Divine guardianship, that the gates of the invisible world shall not prevail against it. *We may or may not be employed as agents in the advancement and defence of the truth of God. Our highest aspirations may be thwarted, our best endeavours may be fruitless, our labour may be spent in vain; but the cause for which we strive is safe, and can never fail. If a work is needful to be done, and we do not succeed in doing it, there will be others found to do it. The work and the workman and the workmaster are alike of God, and if we work as unto Him our reward is sure; we may or may not see the fruit of our labours, but it will be garnered in the garner of the Lord. It is not they who win the highest praise of men that are necessarily doing best the Lord's work, for many of whom the world knows little, and for whom it cares nothing, are prompt to do His will, and, in the courts of heaven,

"They also serve who only stand and wait."

There is this peculiar characteristic, then, of the gospel of Jesus Christ, that it supplies the highest standard by which it can itself be judged. You cannot, from without the area of gospel influence, obtain a higher standard by which it can be measured. And any standard which can be discovered within the moral consciousness,

M

and can be applied to it, has been, if not revealed, at least nurtured and developed by the gospel. The character of Jesus as depicted in the gospels is confessedly unique, not only in the history, but in the literature of the world, and this is the standard by which the gospel must be measured. But it is neither greater nor less than He, for it is Himself.

In human memoirs it is no uncommon thing for the execution of the work to be unworthy of the character portrayed, but this cannot be said of any one of the four gospels, for each serves as a pure and transparent medium, at once to reflect the character and to reveal the presence and reality of the life recorded. In the most artless and unconscious manner each evangelist has drawn a portrait which is unique and unapproachable, and which, after the utmost allowance has been made for variation, is substantially the same.

Nor can it be said that there is any declension or falling off in the epistolary compositions of the New Testament. "Be ye followers of me, as I also am of Christ,"[1] may be taken as expressing their testimony of themselves. And it is just and true. The character of the writer which they reflect, and the insight they give us into the life and character of the first disciples, as well as the precepts they inculcate, are worthy even of the sublime example given by Christ and stereotyped in the gospels. They show that the first effects of regenerate humanity were cognate with the influence which regenerated it. And these effects, though surpassing everything which had been exhibited before, became conceivable after what had been achieved by Christ. He had shown what humanity was capable of, and by the impulse of His victory over death had rendered approximation to it possible.

[1] 1 Cor. xi. 1.

To those, then, who are capable of feeling this there can be no higher evidence of the Divine origin of the gospel. It speaks for itself as by a voice from heaven. To define the limits of the supernatural in the means employed may be a matter of difficulty and delicacy, but about the results produced there can be no reasonable question. If otherwise, we may rest assured that no accumulation of evidence will suffice to produce the conviction of that which is confessedly beyond the reach of demonstration. There is a point where belief becomes an affair of the will rather than of the reason, a matter of the affections rather than the intellect. When that point is reached the function of argument ceases, and that of prayer begins. A man may be beyond the reach of argument, he can never be beyond the power of prayer. He who can be untouched at the spectacle of a brother or a sister praying for him must be more of a fiend than a man. He may disbelieve in prayer, but he must feel humbled before one who prays, and who prays for him.

The regenerating power of the gospel is not more striking in the entirely new literature which was created by it, than it is in the ever new results which that literature is continually producing. It was undeniably the motive power of the reformation, which was itself the greatest moral event since the commencement of Christianity. It is the only power which can cope with the deep-seated strength of Romanism, and it is surely destined to overthrow it. There is nothing that Romanism more instinctively dreads, or for which it has a deeper hatred, than the widespread circulation of the New Testament, and the preaching of the true gospel of Christ. In the long run the gospel may be safely left to make its own way, by bringing before men the person of Christ, and the three cardinal facts of

His life, death, and resurrection. There is much opposition, much enmity, much prejudice, and ignorance to be encountered, but it will ultimately triumph over all. The power it has exercised not only in the life of individuals, but on the life of nations, is too conspicuous to be called in question. The present greatness of England is in a high degree directly traceable to the influence of that literature which was the immediate outcome of faith in Christ, while the life of many a saint would have been impossible without its influence, and is inexplicable except on the supposition of its truth. Is not the life of a Henry Martyn, a John Newton, a William Wilberforce, a Richard Baxter, a Thomas Ken, or a Charles Simeon, a standing witness to the regenerating power of the gospel as well as to the Divine origin to which alone that power can be ascribed? And there are thousands in the present day, unknown and unobserved, who are secretly and silently obeying this power, and thanking God for the influence it exerts upon them. Withdraw from mankind the operation of this influence, obliterate the gospel from their memory, efface its character from their hearts, its results, direct and indirect, from their lives, and the moral consequences would be frightful to contemplate. We should at once relapse into a condition which the apostle justly describes as "having no hope, and without God in the world."[1]

For independently of the moral results on national life and conduct, which may fairly be attributed to the influence of the gospel, there are others of a totally different kind, which it is impossible to gauge or estimate. These are the strength, and courage, and hope, and consolation, and peace, which it has bestowed upon the weak, the timid, the desponding, the sorrowful, the weary. Who shall count the hours of mortal

[1] Ephesians ii. 12.

agony which would have been unendurable but for the faith of the gospel of Jesus Christ? How many a dying pillow has been smoothed by the recollection of His presence, the power of His undying life? How many overwhelming sorrows that have made the heart ache without hope of earthly remedy have been met by the strong consolation of the gospel, when nothing else could meet them? How many gnawings of the conscience, produced by the bitterest of all causes—self-reproach, have been healed, as far as in this life they ever can be healed, by the balm of gospel truth, when if left to work out their own end it could only have been suicide or madness?

And shall we tolerate for one moment the base, unmanly, dishonourable insinuation that this, which is now working day by day and hour by hour in the nineteenth century of its life and light, as nothing else can work, may, after all, possibly not be true. Oh, my brethren! comrades in mortality and sin, let us look this matter bravely in the face, and decide for ourselves once for all whether it is true or false. At all events these visible, palpable results are realities : they cannot be mistaken, they cannot be counterfeited ; and is the cause producing them, the resurrection and eternal life of the Lord Jesus, an unreality ? Is belief in His name a delusion, an enthusiastic dream ? If we determine that it is, then God has indeed not left Himself without witness, but we are they that it can never reach. If the present power of the gospel cannot make itself felt by us, no amount of evidence or argument will suffice to persuade us that it was Divine.

Nor let us ever forget that the real issue is a very simple one. It is possible to cloud that issue in a variety of ways, to perplex and darken it with a multitude of questions which are hopelessly insoluble, and consequently unprofitable ;

but, sooner or later, the root question must be, "Dost thou believe on the Lord Jesus Christ?" That faith must either be partial, or it is infinite. But any faith in Christ that is less than infinite is virtually no faith at all. For true faith in Christ must absorb the whole soul, control the whole life, command the whole will, subdue the whole man. Faith which does not do this is not directed to the central, living, personal object, but is directed to some subordinate, collateral point, which it mistakes for Him; or it is intercepted by some abstract thought which is fatal to the reality of His claims, and destroys the integrity of His person. Jesus Christ has either an absolute right to our allegiance, or He has no right at all. We must either take Him on His own estimate, or we must virtually reject Him. There is not really any middle course to choose. And it is the adoption of this choice which is necessarily involved in our moral responsibility as men to whom the message of the gospel has been brought. We cannot escape from it. We must, sooner or later, determine whether in accepting the message of the gospel we will acknowledge Jesus, or whether in rejecting it we will reject Him. But if we reject Him we reject the only regenerating power which has been given to the world. We cut ourselves off from that life which all who believe in Jesus have surely found in Him. We turn our backs upon those avenues of hope, which lead through darkness, toil, and sorrow, to an infinite and bright futurity. Yea, more, we forego likewise that which bestows the greatest sweetness on, and invests with the highest beauty, the life that now is, for the promise was, " He that followeth me shall not walk in darkness, but shall have the light of life." [1]

In the midst, then, of all the confusions and defects of the existing Church, we turn with

[1] John viii. 12.

delight and with eager hope and confidence to the simple elemental gospel of the life, death, and resurrection of the Lord Jesus. It is this which has so often proved itself Divine, and yet again will do so. There is the essence of all theology, the germ of all life in this. To cling fast to the person of Him who lived and died, and rose again, is to cling fast to God. We cannot have Him with us and not have life. The subsidiary helps of symbolism and of a ritual which appeals immediately to the senses will be superseded by the power of a spiritual union, which is superior to and independent of them. To know the power of the resurrection of Jesus Christ is to rise above the influence of any mere form or tradition of the past to the life and reality of the eternal present, to be indifferent to the expression of outward ceremonial because we grasp in its integrity the central truth which it expresses.

On the other hand, to believe in the life

and death and resurrection of Jesus Christ, is to know the vanity of all boasted science, of all which aspires to supersede and to supplant the faith which was once for all delivered to the saints: it is to know that there is a truer and a better wisdom than to fall down before and worship the fluctuating opinions and theories of men, it is to feel that we rest on fact, and on the Person of a true humanity, which while it excites and satisfies the most boundless aspirations, is at the same time an anchor of the soul both sure and steadfast, to hold us back from drifting into vain imaginings that are incompatible with the truth of Christ. To know that He lived gives a higher zest and charm to life: to know that He died at once tempers joy, and takes away the sting of death; it chastens and corrects our confidence and pride of life; it rebukes and expiates our sin; it sanctifies and moderates our grief: to know that He rose again is to receive health and strength and hope and life from Him, to rejoice in the forgiveness of sins and in the abiding consolation of the Holy Ghost.

And, once more, to live in the power of the historic reality of the life and death and resurrection of Jesus Christ, is to be delivered from the mental thraldom of a merely dogmatic belief in propositions, to be set free from those idols of the forum or the cave which, while they keep the mind in bondage to a traditional and stereotyped form of words, leave the heart destitute of real life, because, instead of feeding it with the living entity, they attempt to satisfy it with the bare expression of a truth which, being spiritual, no words can utter.

It is thus that the simple facts of a gospel of fact, when held in their simplicity and in their vitality, serve to meet at any point the various wants and deficiencies of our existing Christianity, and infusing into it a new stream of pure and heavenly life, present another evidence of its inherent power, and, therefore, of its Divine origin. And thus the gospel of Jesus Christ, when rightly received and earnestly accepted, becomes its own unerring witness, by being now, as it was eighteen centuries ago, to every one that believeth, the power of God unto salvation.[1]

[1] Rom. i. 16.

THE END.

Printed by William Moore & Co.

MAY, 1874.

A CLASSIFIED CATALOGUE OF HENRY S. KING & CO.'S PUBLICATIONS.

CONTENTS.

	PAGE		PAGE
HISTORY AND BIOGRAPHY	1	BOOKS FOR THE YOUNG, &c.	16
VOYAGES AND TRAVEL	4	WORKS OF MR. TENNYSON	19
SCIENCE	6	POETRY	20
ESSAYS, LECTURES, AND COLLECTED PAPERS	10	FICTION	22
		CORNHILL LIBRARY OF FICTION	25
MILITARY WORKS	11	THEOLOGICAL	26
INDIA AND THE EAST	14	MISCELLANEOUS	31

HISTORY AND BIOGRAPHY.

AUTOBIOGRAPHY AND OTHER MEMORIALS OF MRS. GILBERT, FORMERLY ANN TAYLOR. By **Josiah Gilbert,** Author of "The Titian and Cadore Country," &c. In 2 vols. Post 8vo. With Steel Portraits, and several Wood Engravings. [*Preparing.*

AUTOBIOGRAPHY OF DR. A. B. GRANVILLE, M.D., F.R.S., &c. Edited, with a brief account of his concluding years, by his youngest Daughter. 2 vols. Demy 8vo. With a Portrait. [*Preparing.*

SAMUEL LOVER, THE LIFE AND UNPUBLISHED WORKS OF. By **Bayle Bernard.** In 2 vols. Post 8vo. With a Steel Portrait. [*Preparing.*

A MEMOIR OF THE REV. DR. ROWLAND WILLIAMS, with selections from his Note-books and Correspondence. Edited by **Mrs. Rowland Williams.** With a Photographic Portrait. In 2 vols. Large post 8vo. [*Shortly.*

POLITICAL WOMEN. By **Sutherland Menzies.** 2 vols. Post 8vo. Price 24s.

"Has all the information of history, with all the interest that attaches to biography." —*Scotsman.*

"A graceful contribution to the lighter record of history."—*English Churchman.*

65, *Cornhill;* & 12, *Paternoster Row, London.*

HISTORY AND BIOGRAPHY—*continued.*

SARA COLERIDGE, MEMOIR AND LETTERS OF. Edited by her **Daughter.** 2 vols. Crown 8vo. With 2 Portraits. Price 24s. Third Edition, Revised and Corrected. With Index.

"Sara Coleridge, as she is revealed, or rather reveals herself, in the correspondence, makes a brilliant addition to a brilliant family reputation."—*Saturday Review.*

"These charming volumes are attractive as a memorial of a most amiable woman of high intellectual mark."—*Athenæum.*
"We have read these two volumes with genuine gratification."—*Hour.*

THE LATE REV. F. W. ROBERTSON, M.A., LIFE AND LETTERS OF. Edited by **Stopford Brooke, M.A.**, Chaplain in Ordinary to the Queen.
   I. In 2 vols., uniform with the Sermons. Price 7s. 6d.
   II. Library Edition, in demy 8vo, with Two Steel Portraits. Price 12s.
   III. A Popular Edition, in 1 vol. Price 6s.

NATHANIEL HAWTHORNE, A MEMOIR OF, with Stories now first published in this country. By **H. A. Page.** Large post 8vo. 7s. 6d.

"Seldom has it been our lot to meet with a more appreciative delineation of character than this Memoir of Hawthorne."—*Morning Post.*

"Exhibits a discriminating enthusiasm for one of the most fascinating of novelists."—*Saturday Review.*

LEONORA CHRISTINA, MEMOIRS OF, Daughter of Christian IV. of Denmark: Written during her Imprisonment in the Blue Tower of the Royal Palace at Copenhagen, 1663—1685. Translated by **F. E. Bunnett.** With an Autotype Portrait of the Princess. Medium 8vo. 12s. 6d.

"A valuable addition to history."—*Daily News.*

"A valuable addition to the tragic romance of history."—*Spectator.*

LIVES OF ENGLISH POPULAR LEADERS. No. 1.—STEPHEN LANGTON. By **C. Edmund Maurice.** Crown 8vo. 7s. 6d.

CABINET PORTRAITS. BIOGRAPHICAL SKETCHES OF STATESMEN OF THE DAY. By **T. Wemyss Reid.** 1 vol. Crown 8vo. 7s. 6d.

"We have never met with a work which we can more unreservedly praise. The sketches are absolutely impartial."—*Athenæum.*

"We can heartily commend this work."—*Standard.*
"Drawn with a master hand."—*Yorkshire Post.*

THE CHURCH AND THE EMPIRES: Historical Periods. By the late **Henry W. Wilberforce.** Preceded by a Memoir of the Author by the **Rev. John Henry Newman, D.D.** 1 vol. Post 8vo. With a Portrait. Price 10s. 6d.

HISTORY OF THE ENGLISH REVOLUTION OF 1688. By **C. D. Yonge,** Regius Professor, Queen's Coll., Belfast. 1 vol. Crown 8vo. Price 6s.

ALEXIS DE TOCQUEVILLE. Correspondence and Conversations with NASSAU W. SENIOR, from 1833 to 1859. Edited by **Mrs. M. C. M. Simpson.** In 2 vols. Large post 8vo. 21s.

"A book replete with knowledge and thought."—*Quarterly Review.*

"An extremely interesting book."—*Saturday Review.*

Works Published by Henry S. King & Co., 3

HISTORY AND BIOGRAPHY—*continued*.

JOURNALS KEPT IN FRANCE AND ITALY. From 1848 to 1852. With a Sketch of the Revolution of 1848. By the late **Nassau William Senior**. Edited by his Daughter, **M. C. M. Simpson**. In 2 vols. Post 8vo. 24*s*.

"The book has a genuine historical value."—*Saturday Review*.
"No better, more honest, and more readable view of the state of political society during the existence of the second Republic could well be looked for."—*Examiner*.

PERSIA; ANCIENT AND MODERN. By **John Piggot, F.S.A.** Post 8vo. Price 10*s*. 6*d*.

THE HISTORY OF JAPAN. From the Earliest Period to the Present Time. By **Francis Ottiwell Adams**, H.B.M.'s Secretary of Embassy at Berlin, formerly H.B.M.'s Chargé d'Affaires, and Secretary of Legation at Yedo. Demy 8vo. With Map and Plans. Price 21*s*.

THE NORMAN PEOPLE, AND THEIR EXISTING DESCENDANTS IN THE BRITISH DOMINIONS AND THE UNITED STATES OF AMERICA. One handsome vol. 8vo. Price 21*s*.

THE RUSSIANS IN CENTRAL ASIA. A Critical Examination, down to the present time, of the Geography and History of Central Asia. By **Baron F. von Hellwald**. Translated by **Lieut.-Col. Theodore Wirgman, LL.B.** In 1 vol. Large post 8vo, with Map. Price 12*s*.

BOKHARA: ITS HISTORY AND CONQUEST. By **Professor Arminius Vàmbèry**, of the University of Pesth, Author of "Travels in Central Asia," &c. Demy 8vo. Price 18*s*.

"We conclude with a cordial recommendation of this valuable book."—*Saturday Review*.
"Almost every page abounds with composition of peculiar merit."—*Morning Post*.

THE RELIGIOUS HISTORY OF IRELAND: PRIMITIVE, PAPAL, AND PROTESTANT; including the Evangelical Missions, Catholic Agitations, and Church Progress of the last half Century. By **James Godkin**, Author of "Ireland: her Churches," &c. 1 vol. 8vo. Price 12*s*.

"These latter chapters on the statistics of the various religious denominations will be welcomed."—*Evening Standard*.
"Mr. Godkin writes with evident honesty, and the topic on which he writes is one about which an honest book is greatly wanted."—*Examiner*.

THE GOVERNMENT OF THE NATIONAL DEFENCE. From the 30th June to the 31st October, 1870. The Plain Statement of a Member. By **Mons. Jules Favre**. 1 vol. Demy 8vo. 10*s*. 6*d*.

"Of all the contributions to the history of the late war, we have found none more fascinating and, perhaps, none more valuable than the 'apology,' by M. Jules Favre, for the unsuccessful Government of the National Defence."—*Times*.
"A work of the highest interest. The book is most valuable."—*Athenæum*.

ECHOES OF A FAMOUS YEAR. By **Harriet Parr**, Author of "The Life of Jeanne d'Arc," "In the Silver Age," &c. Crown 8vo. 8*s*. 6*d*.

"Miss Parr has the great gift of charming simplicity of style; and if children are not interested in her book, many of their seniors will be."—*British Quarterly Review*.

65, *Cornhill*; & 12, *Paternoster Row, London*.

VOYAGES AND TRAVEL.

SOME TIME IN IRELAND; A Recollection. 1 vol. Crown 8vo.
[*Preparing.*

WAYSIDE NOTES IN SCANDINAVIA. Being Notes of Travel in the North of Europe. By **Mark Antony Lower, M.A.** 1 vol. Crown 8vo.
[*Preparing.*

ON THE ROAD TO KHIVA. By **David Ker**, late Khivan Correspondent of the *Daily Telegraph*. Illustrated with Photographs of the Country and its Inhabitants, and a copy of the Official Map in use during the Campaign, from the Survey of CAPTAIN LEUSILIN. 1 vol. Post 8vo.   12s.

VIZCAYA; or, Life in the land of the Carlists at the outbreak of the Insurrection, with some account of the Iron Mines and other characteristics of the country. With a Map and 8 Illustrations. Crown 8vo.   [*Just ready.*

ROUGH NOTES OF A VISIT TO BELGIUM, SEDAN, AND PARIS, in September, 1870-71. By **John Ashton.** Crown 8vo, bevelled boards. Price 3s. 6d.

"The author does not attempt to deal with military subjects, but writes sensibly of what he saw in 1870-71."—*John Bull.*
"Possesses a certain freshness from the straightforward simplicity with which it is written."—*Graphic.*
"An interesting work by a highly intelligent observer."—*Standard.*

THE ALPS OF ARABIA; or, Travels through Egypt, Sinai, Arabia, and the Holy Land. By **William Charles Maughan.** 1 vol. Demy 8vo, with Map. Price 12s.

"Deeply interesting and valuable."—*Edinburgh Review.*
"He writes freshly and with competent knowledge."—*Standard.*
"Very readable and instructive.... A work far above the average of such publications."—*John Bull.*

THE MISHMEE HILLS: an Account of a Journey made in an Attempt to Penetrate Thibet from Assam, to open New Routes for Commerce. By **T. T. Cooper**, Author of "The Travels of a Pioneer of Commerce." Demy 8vo. With Four Illustrations and Map. Price 10s. 6d.

"The volume, which will be of great use in India and among Indian merchants here, contains a good deal of matter that will interest ordinary readers. It is especially rich in sporting incidents."—*Standard.*

GOODMAN'S CUBA, THE PEARL OF THE ANTILLES. By **Walter Goodman.** Crown 8vo. Price 7s. 6d.

"A series of vivid and miscellaneous sketches. We can recommend this whole volume as very amusing reading."—*Pall Mall Gazette.*
"The whole book deserves the heartiest commendation... Sparkling and amusing from beginning to end."—*Spectator.*

FIELD AND FOREST RAMBLES OF A NATURALIST IN NEW BRUNSWICK. With Notes and Observations on the Natural History of Eastern Canada. By **A. Leith Adams, M.A.** In 8vo, cloth. Illustrated. Price 14s.

"Both sportsmen and naturalists will find this work replete with anecdote and carefully-recorded observation, which will entertain them."—*Nature.*
"Will be found interesting by those who take a pleasure either in sport or natural history."—*Athenæum.*
"To the naturalist the book will be most valuable... To the general reader most interesting."—*Evening Standard.*

ROUND THE WORLD IN 1870. A Volume of Travels, with Maps. By **A. D. Carlisle, B.A.**, Trin. Coll., Camb. Demy 8vo. Price 16s.

"We can only commend, which we do very heartily, an eminently sensible and readable book."—*British Quarterly Review.*

VOYAGES AND TRAVEL—*continued*.

TENT LIFE WITH ENGLISH GIPSIES IN NORWAY. By **Hubert Smith.** In 8vo, cloth. Five full-page Engravings, and 31 smaller Illustrations, with Map of the Country showing Routes. Second Edition. Revised and Corrected. Price 21*s*.

"Written in a very lively style, and has throughout a smack of dry humour and satiric reflection which the writer to be a keen observer of men and things. We hope that many will read it and find in it the same amusement as ourselves."—*Times*.

FAYOUM; OR, ARTISTS IN EGYPT. A Tour with M. Gérôme and others. By **J. Lenoir.** Crown 8vo, cloth. Illustrated. Price 7*s*. 6*d*.

"A pleasantly written and very readable book."—*Examiner*.
"The book is very amusing. . . . Who-ever may take it up will find he has with him a bright and pleasant companion."—*Spectator*.

SPITZBERGEN THE GATEWAY TO THE POLYNIA; OR, A VOYAGE TO SPITZBERGEN. By **Captain John C. Wells, R.N.** In 8vo, cloth. Profusely Illustrated. Price 21*s*.

"A charming book, remarkably well written and well illustrated."—*Standard*.
"Straightforward and clear in style, securing our confidence by its unaffected simplicity and good sense."—*Saturday Review*.

AN AUTUMN TOUR IN THE UNITED STATES AND CANADA. By **Lieut.-Col. J. G. Medley.** Crown 8vo. Price 5*s*.

"Colonel Medley's little volume is a pleasantly written account of a two-months' visit to America."—*Hour*.
"May be recommended as manly, sensible, and pleasantly written."—*Globe*.

THE NILE WITHOUT A DRAGOMAN. By **Frederic Eden.** Second Edition. In 1 vol. Crown 8vo, cloth. Price 7*s*. 6*d*.

"Should any of our readers care to imitate Mr. Eden's example, and wish to see things with their own eyes, and shift for themselves, next winter in Upper Egypt, they will find this book a very agreeable guide."—*Times*.
"It is a book to read during an autumn holiday."—*Spectator*.

IRELAND IN 1872. A Tour of Observation, with Remarks on Irish Public Questions. By **Dr. James Macaulay.** Crown 8vo. Price 7*s*. 6*d*.

"A careful and instructive book. Full of facts, full of information, and full of interest."—*Literary Churchman*.
"We have rarely met a book on Ireland which for impartiality of criticism and general accuracy of information could be so well recommended to the fair-minded Irish reader."—*Evening Standard*.

OVER THE DOVREFJELDS. By **J. S. Shepard,** Author of "A Ramble through Norway," &c. Crown 8vo. Illustrated. Price 4*s*. 6*d*.

"We have read many books of Norwegian travel, but . . . we have seen none so pleasantly narrative in its style, and so varied in its subject."—*Spectator*.
"As interesting a little volume as could be written on the subject. So interesting and shortly written that it will commend itself to all intending tourists."—*Examiner*.

A WINTER IN MOROCCO. By **Amelia Perrier.** Large crown 8vo. Illustrated. Price 10*s*. 6*d*.

"Well worth reading, and contains several excellent illustrations."—*Hour*.
"Miss Perrier is a very amusing writer. She has a good deal of humour, sees the oddity and quaintness of Oriental life with a quick observant eye, and evidently turned her opportunities of sarcastic examination to account."—*Daily News*.

THE QUESTIONS OF AURAL SURGERY. By James Hinton, Aural Surgeon to Guy's Hospital. Post 8vo. Price 12s. 6d.

AN ATLAS OF DISEASES OF THE MEMBRANA TYMPANI. With Descriptive Text. By **James Hinton**, Aural Surgeon to Guy's Hospital. Post 8vo. Price £6 6s.

PHYSIOLOGY FOR PRACTICAL USE. By various Writers. Edited by **James Hinton**. 2 vols. Crown 8vo. With 50 Illustrations. 12s. 6d.

THE PRINCIPLES OF MENTAL PHYSIOLOGY. With their Applications to the Training and Discipline of the Mind, and the Study of its Morbid Conditions. By **W. B. Carpenter, LL.D., M.D., F.R.S.**, &c. 8vo. Illustrated. Price 12s.

SENSATION AND INTUITION. By **James Sully**. 1 vol. Post 8vo. [*Nearly ready*.

THE EXPANSE OF HEAVEN. A Series of Essays on the Wonders of the Firmament. By **R. A. Proctor, B.A.** Second Edition. With a Frontispiece. Small crown 8vo. Price 6s.

"A very charming work; cannot fail to lift the reader's mind up 'through nature's work to nature's God.'"—*Standard.*

" Full of thought, readable, and popular." —*Brighton Gazette.*

STUDIES OF BLAST FURNACE PHENOMENA. By **M. L. Gruner.** Translated by **L. D. B. Gordon, F.R.S.E., F.G.S.**, &c. Demy 8vo. Price 7s. 6d.

"The whole subject is dealt with very copiously and clearly in all its parts, and can scarcely fail of appreciation at the hands of practical men, for whose use it is designed."—*Post.*

A LEGAL HANDBOOK FOR ARCHITECTS. By **Edward Jenkins** and **John Raymond, Esqrs.**, Barristers-at-Law. In 1 vol. Price 6s.

"Architects, builders, and especially the building public will find the volume very useful."—*Freeman.*

"We can confidently recommend this book to all engaged in the building trades."—*Edinburgh Daily Review.*

CONTEMPORARY ENGLISH PSYCHOLOGY. From the French of **Professor Th. Ribot.** Large post 8vo. Price 9s. An Analysis of the Views and Opinions of the following Metaphysicians, as expressed in their writings:—

JAMES MILL, A. BAIN, JOHN STUART MILL, GEORGE H. LEWES, HERBERT SPENCER, SAMUEL BAILEY.

THE HISTORY OF CREATION, a Popular Account of the Development of the Earth and its Inhabitants, according to the theories of Kant, Laplace, Lamarck, and Darwin. By **Professor Ernst Hæckel**, of the University of Jena. With Coloured Plates and Genealogical Trees of the various groups of both plants and animals. 2 vols. Post 8vo. [*Preparing.*

SCIENCE—*continued*.

A New Edition.

CHANGE OF AIR AND SCENE. A Physician's Hints about Doctors, Patients, Hygiène, and Society; with Notes of Excursions for health in the Pyrenees, and amongst the Watering-places of France (Inland and Seaward), Switzerland, Corsica, and the Mediterranean. By **Dr. Alphonse Donné.** Large post 8vo. Price 9s.

"A very readable and serviceable book. ... The real value of it is to be found in the accurate and minute information given with regard to a large number of places which have gained a reputation on the continent for their mineral waters."—*Pall Mall Gazette*.
"A singularly pleasant and chatty as well as instructive book about health."—*Guardian*.

MISS YOUMANS' FIRST BOOK OF BOTANY. Designed to cultivate the observing powers of Children. From the Author's latest Stereotyped Edition. New and Enlarged Edition, with 300 Engravings. Crown 8vo. Price 5s.

"It is but rarely that a school-book appears which is at once so novel in plan, so successful in execution, and so suited to the general want, as to command universal and unqualified approbation, but such has been the case with Miss Youmans' First Book of Botany. ... It has been everywhere welcomed as a timely and invaluable contribution to the improvement of primary education."—*Pall Mall Gazette*.

AN ARABIC AND ENGLISH DICTIONARY OF THE KORAN. By **Major J. Penrice, B.A.** 4to. Price 21s.

MODERN GOTHIC ARCHITECTURE. By **T. G. Jackson.** Crown 8vo. Price 5s.

"This thoughtful little book is worthy of the perusal of all interested in art or architecture."—*Standard*.
"The reader will find some of the most important doctrines of eminent art teachers practically applied in this little book, which is well written and popular in style."—*Manchester Examiner*.

A TREATISE ON RELAPSING FEVER. By **R. T. Lyons,** Assistant-Surgeon, Bengal Army. Small post 8vo. Price 7s. 6d.

"A practical work, thoroughly supported in its views by a series of remarkable cases."—*Standard*.

FOUR WORKS BY DR. EDWARD SMITH.

I. HEALTH AND DISEASE, as influenced by the Daily, Seasonal, and other Cyclical Changes in the Human System. A New Edition. Price 7s. 6d.

II. FOODS. Second Edition. Profusely Illustrated. Price 5s.

III. PRACTICAL DIETARY FOR FAMILIES, SCHOOLS, AND THE LABOURING CLASSES. A New Edition. Price 3s. 6d.

IV. CONSUMPTION IN ITS EARLY AND REMEDIABLE STAGES. A New Edition. Price 7s. 6d.

CHOLERA: HOW TO AVOID AND TREAT IT. Popular and Practical Notes by **Henry Blanc, M.D.** Crown 8vo. Price 4s. 6d.

"A very practical manual, based on experience and careful observation, full of excellent hints on a most dangerous disease."—*Standard*.

SCIENCE—*continued.*

THE INTERNATIONAL SCIENTIFIC SERIES.

Fourth Edition.

I. **THE FORMS OF WATER IN RAIN AND RIVERS, ICE AND GLACIERS.** By **J. Tyndall, LL.D., F.R.S.** With 26 Illustrations. Crown 8vo. Price 5s.

Second Edition.

II. **PHYSICS AND POLITICS**; OR, THOUGHTS ON THE APPLICATION OF THE PRINCIPLES OF "NATURAL SELECTION" AND "INHERITANCE" TO POLITICAL SOCIETY. By **Walter Bagehot.** Crown 8vo. Price 4s.

Third Edition.

III. **FOODS.** By **Dr. Edward Smith.** Profusely Illustrated. Price 5s.

Third Edition.

IV. **MIND AND BODY**: THE THEORIES OF THEIR RELATIONS. By **Alexander Bain, LL.D.**, Professor of Logic at the University of Aberdeen. Four Illustrations. Price 4s.

Third Edition.

V. **THE STUDY OF SOCIOLOGY.** By **Herbert Spencer.** Crown 8vo. Price 5s.

Second Edition.

VI. **ON THE CONSERVATION OF ENERGY.** By **Professor Balfour Stewart.** Fourteen Engravings. Price 5s.

Second Edition.

VII. **ANIMAL LOCOMOTION**; or, Walking, Swimming, and Flying. By **Dr. J. B. Pettigrew, M.D., F.R.S.** 119 Illustrations. Price 5s.

Second Edition.

VIII. **RESPONSIBILITY IN MENTAL DISEASE.** By **Dr. Henry Maudsley.** Price 5s.

Second Edition.

IX. **THE NEW CHEMISTRY.** By **Professor Josiah P. Cooke**, of the Harvard University. Illustrated. Price 5s.

X. **THE SCIENCE OF LAW.** By **Professor Sheldon Amos.**
[*Just ready.*

The International Scientific Series—*continued.*

FORTHCOMING VOLUMES.

Prof. E. J. MAREY.
   The Animal Frame. [*In the Press.*

Prof. OSCAR SCHMIDT (Strasburg Univ.).
   The Theory of Descent and Darwinism. [*In the Press.*

Prof. VOGEL (Polytechnic Acad. of Berlin).
   The Chemical Effects of Light. [*In the Press.*

Prof. LONMEL (University of Erlangen).
   Optics. [*In the Press.*

{ Rev. M. J. BERKELEY, M.A., F.L.S.,
  and M. COOKE, M.A., LL.D.
   Fungi; their Nature, Influences, and Uses.

Prof. W. KINGDOM CLIFFORD, M.A.
   The First Principles of the Exact Sciences explained to the non-mathematical.

Prof. T. H. HUXLEY, LL.D., F.R.S.
   Bodily Motion and Consciousness.

Dr. W. B. CARPENTER, LL.D., F.R.S.
   The Physical Geography of the Sea.

Prof. WILLIAM ODLING, F.R.S.
   The Old Chemistry viewed from the new Standpoint.

W. LAUDER LINDSAY, M.D., F.R.S.E.
   Mind in the Lower Animals.

Sir JOHN LUBBOCK, Bart., F.R.S.
   The Antiquity of Man.

Prof. W. T. THISELTON DYER, B.A., B.SC.
   Form and Habit in Flowering Plants.

Mr. J. N. LOCKYER, F.R.S.
   Spectrum Analysis.

Prof. MICHAEL FOSTER, M.D.
   Protoplasm and the Cell Theory.

Prof. W. STANLEY JEVONS.
   Money: and the Mechanism of Exchange.

Dr. H. CHARLTON BASTIAN, M.D., F.R.S.
   The Brain as an Organ of Mind.

Prof. A. C. RAMSAY, LL.D., F.R.S.
   Earth Sculpture: Hills, Valleys, Mountains, Plains, Rivers, Lakes; how they were Produced, and how they have been Destroyed.

Prof. RUDOLPH VIRCHOW (Berlin Univ.)
   Morbid Physiological Action.

Prof. CLAUDE BERNARD.
   Physical and Metaphysical Phenomena of Life.

Prof. H. SAINTE-CLAIRE DEVILLE.
   An Introduction to General Chemistry.

Prof. WURTZ.
   Atoms and the Atomic Theory.

Prof. DE QUATREFAGES.
   The Negro Races.

Prof. LACAZE-DUTHIERS.
   Zoology since Cuvier.

Prof. BERTHELOT.
   Chemical Synthesis.

Prof. J. ROSENTHAL.
   General Physiology of Muscles and Nerves.

Prof. JAMES D. DANA, M.A., LL.D.
   On Cephalization; or, Head-Characters in the Gradation and Progress of Life.

Prof. S. W. JOHNSON, M.A.
   On the Nutrition of Plants.

Prof. AUSTIN FLINT, Jr. M.D.
   The Nervous System and its Relation to the Bodily Functions.

Prof. W. D. WHITNEY.
   Modern Linguistic Science.

Prof. BERNSTEIN (University of Halle).
   Physiology of the Senses.

Prof. FERDINAND COHN (Breslau Univ.).
   Thallophytes (Algæ, Lichens, Fungi).

Prof. HERMANN (University of Zurich).
   Respiration.

Prof. LEUCKART (University of Leipsic).
   Outlines of Animal Organization.

Prof. LIEBREICH (University of Berlin).
   Outlines of Toxicology.

Prof. KUNDT (University of Strasburg).
   On Sound.

Prof. REES (University of Erlangen).
   On Parasitic Plants.

Prof. STEINTHAL (University of Berlin).
   Outlines of the Science of Language.

ESSAYS, LECTURES, AND COLLECTED PAPERS.

IN STRANGE COMPANY; or, The Note Book of a Roving Correspondent. By **James Greenwood**, "The Amateur Casual." Second Edition. Crown 8vo. 6s.

"A bright, lively book."—*Standard.*
"Has all the interest of romance."—*Queen.*

"Some of the papers remind us of Charles Lamb on beggars and chimney sweeps."—*Echo.*

MASTER-SPIRITS. By **Robert Buchanan**. Post 8vo. 10s. 6d.

"Good Books are the precious life-blood of Master-Spirits."—*Milton.*

"Full of fresh and vigorous writing, such as can only be produced by a man of keen and independent intellect."—*Saturday Review.*
"A very pleasant and readable book."—*Examiner.*

"Written with a beauty of language and a spirit of vigorous enthusiasm rare even in our best living word-painters."—*Standard.*
"Mr. Buchanan is a writer whose books the critics may always open with satisfaction . . . both manly and artistic."—*Hour.*

THEOLOGY IN THE ENGLISH POETS; COWPER, COLERIDGE, WORDSWORTH, and BURNS. Being Lectures delivered by the **Rev. Stopford A. Brooke**, Chaplain in Ordinary to Her Majesty the Queen. Crown 8vo. 9s.

SHORT LECTURES ON THE LAND LAWS. Delivered before the Working Men's College. By **T. Lean Wilkinson**. Crown 8vo, limp cloth. 2s.

"A very handy and intelligible epitome of the general principles of existing land laws."—*Standard.*

AN ESSAY ON THE CULTURE OF THE OBSERVING POWERS OF CHILDREN, especially in connection with the Study of Botany. By **Eliza A. Youmans**. Edited, with Notes and a Supplement, by **Joseph Payne, F.C.P.**, Author of "Lectures on the Science and Art of Education," &c. Crown 8vo. 2s. 6d.

"This study, according to her just notions on the subject, is to be fundamentally based on the exercise of the pupil's own powers of observation. He is to see and examine the properties of plants and flowers at first hand, not merely to be informed of what others have seen and examined."—*Pall Mall Gazette.*

THE GENIUS OF CHRISTIANITY UNVEILED. Being Essays by **William Godwin**, Author of "Political Justice," &c. Never before published. 1 vol. Crown 8vo. 7s. 6d.

"Few have thought more clearly and directly than William Godwin, or expressed their reflections with more simplicity and unreserve."—*Examiner.*

"The deliberate thoughts of Godwin deserve to be put before the world for reading and consideration."—*Athenæum.*

MILITARY WORKS.

RUSSIA'S ADVANCE EASTWARD; Translated from the German of LIEUT. STUMM. By **Lt. C. E. H. Vincent.** 1 vol. Crown 8vo. With a Map.

THE VOLUNTEER, THE MILITIAMAN, AND THE REGULAR SOLDIER; a Conservative View of the Armies of England, Past, Present, and Future, as Seen in January, 1874. By **A Public School Boy.** 1 vol. Crown 8vo.

THE OPERATIONS OF THE FIRST ARMY, UNDER STEINMETZ. By **Major von Schell.** Translated by **Captain E. O. Hollist.** Demy 8vo. Uniform with the other volumes in the Series. Price 10s. 6d.

THE OPERATIONS OF THE FIRST ARMY UNDER GEN. VON GOEBEN. By **Major von Schell.** Translated by **Col. C. H. von Wright.** Four Maps. Demy 8vo. Price 9s.

THE OPERATIONS OF THE FIRST ARMY IN NORTHERN FRANCE AGAINST FAIDHERBE. By **Colonel Count Hermann von Wartensleben,** Chief of the Staff of the First Army. Translated by **Colonel C. H. von Wright.** In demy 8vo. Uniform with the above. Price 9s.

"Very clear, simple, yet eminently instructive, is this history. It is not overladen with useless details, is written in good taste, and possesses the inestimable value of being in great measure the record of operations actually witnessed by the author, supplemented by official documents."—*Athenæum.*

THE GERMAN ARTILLERY IN THE BATTLES NEAR METZ. Based on the official reports of the German Artillery. By **Captain Hoffbauer,** Instructor in the German Artillery and Engineer School. Translated by **Capt. E. O. Hollist.** [*Preparing.*

THE OPERATIONS OF THE BAVARIAN ARMY CORPS. By **Captain Hugo Helvig.** Translated by **Captain G. S. Schwabe.** With 5 large Maps. Demy 8vo. In 2 vols. Price 24s. Uniform with the other Books in the Series.

AUSTRIAN CAVALRY EXERCISE. From an Abridged Edition compiled by CAPTAIN ILLIA WOINOVITS, of the General Staff, on the Tactical Regulations of the Austrian Army, and prefaced by a General Sketch of the Organisation, &c., of the Country. Translated by **Captain W. S. Cooke.** Crown 8vo, cloth. Price 7s.

History of the Organisation, Equipment, and War Services of

THE REGIMENT OF BENGAL ARTILLERY. Compiled from Published Official and other Records, and various private sources, by **Major Francis W. Stubbs,** Royal (late Bengal) Artillery. Vol. I. will contain WAR SERVICES. The Second Volume will be published separately, and will contain the HISTORY OF THE ORGANISATION AND EQUIPMENT OF THE REGIMENT. In 2 vols. 8vo. With Maps and Plans. [*Preparing.*

65, Cornhill; & 12, Paternoster Row, London.

MILITARY WORKS—*continued.*

VICTORIES AND DEFEATS. An Attempt to explain the Causes which have led to them. An Officer's Manual. By **Col. R. P. Anderson.** Demy 8vo. Price 14s.

"The present book proves that he is a diligent student of military history, his illustrations ranging over a wide field, and including ancient and modern Indian and European warfare."—*Standard.*

"The young officer should have it always at hand to open anywhere and read a bit, and we warrant him that let that bit be ever so small it will give him material for an hour's thinking."—*United Service Gazette.*

THE FRONTAL ATTACK OF INFANTRY. By **Capt. Laymann,** Instructor of Tactics at the Military College, Neisse. Translated by **Colonel Edward Newdigate.** Crown 8vo, limp cloth. Price 2s. 6d.

"An exceedingly useful kind of book. A valuable acquisition to the military student's library. It recounts, in the first place, the opinions and tactical formations which regulated the German army during the early battles of the late war; explains how these were modified in the course of the campaign by the terrible and unanticipated effect of the fire; and how, accordingly, troops should be trained to attack in future wars."—*Naval and Military Gazette.*

ELEMENTARY MILITARY GEOGRAPHY, RECONNOITRING, AND SKETCHING. Compiled for Non-Commissioned Officers and Soldiers of all Arms. By **Lieut. C. E. H. Vincent,** Royal Welsh Fusiliers. Small crown 8vo. Price 2s. 6d.

"This manual takes into view the necessity of every soldier knowing how to read a military map, in order to know to what points in an enemy's country to direct his attention; and provides for this necessity by giving, in terse and sensible language, definitions of varieties of ground and the advantages they present in warfare, together with a number of useful hints in military sketching."—*Naval and Military Gazette.*

THREE WORKS BY LIEUT.-COL. THE HON. A. ANSON, V.C., M.P.

THE ABOLITION OF PURCHASE AND THE ARMY REGULATION BILL OF 1871. Crown 8vo. Price One Shilling.

ARMY RESERVES AND MILITIA REFORMS. Crown 8vo. Sewed. Price One Shilling.

THE STORY OF THE SUPERSESSIONS. Crown 8vo. Price Sixpence.

STUDIES IN THE NEW INFANTRY TACTICS. Parts I. & II. By **Major W. von Schereff.** Translated from the German by **Col. Lumley Graham.** Price 7s. 6d.

"The subject of the respective advantages of attack and defence, and of the methods in which each form of battle should be carried out under the fire of modern arms, is exhaustively and admirably treated; indeed, we cannot but consider it to be decidedly superior to any work which has hitherto appeared in English upon this all-important subject."—*Standard.*

Second Edition. Revised and Corrected.

TACTICAL DEDUCTIONS FROM THE WAR OF 1870—71. By **Captain A. von Boguslawski.** Translated by **Colonel Lumley Graham,** late 18th (Royal Irish) Regiment. Demy 8vo. Uniform with the above. Price 7s.

"We must, without delay, impress brain and forethought into the British Service; and we cannot commence the good work too soon, or better, than by placing the two books ('The Operations of the German Armies' and 'Tactical Deductions') we have here criticised, in every military library, and introducing them as class-books in every tactical school."—*United Service Gazette.*

THE OPERATIONS OF THE SOUTH ARMY IN JANUARY AND FEBRUARY, 1871. Compiled from the Official War Documents of the Head-quarters of the Southern Army. By **Count Hermann von Wartensleben,** Colonel in the Prussian General Staff. Translated by **Colonel C. H. von Wright.** Demy 8vo, with Maps. Uniform with the above. Price 6s.

55, *Cornhill;* & 12, *Paternoster Row, London.*

MILITARY WORKS—*continued*.

THE ARMY OF THE NORTH-GERMAN CONFEDERATION.
A Brief Description of its Organisation, of the different Branches of the Service and their "Rôle" in War, of its Mode of Fighting, &c. By a **Prussian General**. Translated from the German by **Col. Edward Newdigate**. Demy 8vo. Price 5s.

"The work is quite essential to the full use of the other volumes of the 'German Military Series,' which Messrs. King are now producing in handsome uniform style."—*United Service Magazine*.

"Every page of the book deserves attentive study.... The information given on mobilisation, garrison troops, keeping up establishment during war, and on the employment of the different branches of the service, is of great value."—*Standard*.

THE OPERATIONS OF THE GERMAN ARMIES IN FRANCE, FROM SEDAN TO THE END OF THE WAR OF 1870-71.
With Large Official Map. From the Journals of the Head-quarters Staff, by **Major Wm. Blume**. Translated by **E. M. Jones**, Major 20th Foot, late Professor of Military History, Sandhurst. Demy 8vo. Price 9s.

"The book is of absolute necessity to the military student.... The work is one of high merit."—*United Service Gazette*.

"The work of Major von Blume in its English dress forms the most valuable addition to our stock of works upon the war that our press has put forth. Our space forbids our doing more than commending it earnestly as the most authentic and instructive narrative of the second section of the war that has yet appeared."—*Saturday Review*.

HASTY INTRENCHMENTS.
By **Colonel A. Brialmont**. Translated by **Lieutenant Charles A. Empson, R.A.** Demy 8vo. Nine Plates. Price 6s.

"A valuable contribution to military literature."—*Athenæum*.

"In seven short chapters it gives plain directions for forming shelter-trenches, with the best method of carrying the necessary tools, and it offers practical illustrations of the use of hasty intrenchments on the field of battle."—*United Service Magazine*.

"It supplies that which our own text-books give but imperfectly, viz., hints as to how a position can best be strengthened by means ... of such extemporised intrenchments and batteries as can be thrown up by infantry in the space of four or five hours ... deserves to become a standard military work."—*Standard*.

STUDIES IN LEADING TROOPS.
By **Colonel von Verdy Du Vernois**. An authorised and accurate Translation by **Lieutenant H. J. T. Hildyard**, 71st Foot. Parts I. and II. Demy 8vo. Price 7s.

* General BEAUCHAMP WALKER says of this work:—"I recommend the first two numbers of Colonel von Verdy's 'Studies' to the attentive perusal of my brother officers. They supply a want which I have often felt during my service in this country, namely, a minuter tactical detail of the minor operations of war than any but the most observant and fortunately-placed staff-officer is in a position to give. I have read and re-read them very carefully, I hope with profit, certainly with great interest, and believe that practice, in the sense of these 'Studies,' would be a valuable preparation for manœuvres on a more extended scale."—Berlin, June, 1872.

CAVALRY FIELD DUTY.
By **Major-General von Mirus**. Translated by **Captain Frank S. Russell**, 14th (King's) Hussars. Crown 8vo, limp cloth. Price 7s. 6d.

DISCIPLINE AND DRILL.
Four Lectures delivered to the London Scottish Rifle Volunteers. By **Captain S. Flood Page**. A New and Cheaper Edition. Price 1s.

"An admirable collection of lectures."—*Times*.

"The very useful and interesting work."—*Volunteer Service Gazette*.

INDIA AND THE EAST.

THE THREATENED FAMINE IN BENGAL; How it may be Met, and the Recurrence of Famines in India prevented. Being No. 1 of "Occasional Notes on Indian Affairs." By **Sir H. Bartle E. Frere, G.C.B., G.C.S.I.,** &c. &c. Crown 8vo. With 3 Maps. Price 5s.

THE ORIENTAL SPORTING MAGAZINE. A Reprint of the first 5 Volumes, in 2 Volumes, demy 8vo. Price 28s.

"Lovers of sport will find ample amusement in the varied contents of these two volumes."—*Allen's Indian Mail.*

"Full of interest for the sportsman and naturalist. Full of thrilling adventures of sportsmen who have attacked the fiercest and most gigantic specimens of the animal world in their native jungle. It is seldom we get so many exciting incidents in a similar amount of space ... Well suited to the libraries of country gentlemen and all those who are interested in sporting matters."—*Civil Service Gazette.*

THE EUROPEAN IN INDIA. A Hand-book of Practical Information for those proceeding to, or residing in, the East Indies, relating to Outfits, Routes, Time for Departure, Indian Climate, &c. By **Edmund C. P. Hull.** With a MEDICAL GUIDE for ANGLO-INDIANS. Being a Compendium of Advice to Europeans in India, relating to the Preservation and Regulation of Health. By **R. S. Mair, M.D., F.R.C.S.E.,** late Deputy Coroner of Madras. In 1 vol. Post 8vo. Price 6s.

"Full of all sorts of useful information to the English settler or traveller in India."—*Standard.*

"One of the most valuable books ever published in India—valuable for its sound information, its careful array of pertinent facts, and its sterling common sense. It supplies a want which few persons may have discovered, but which everybody will at once recognise when once the contents of the book have been mastered. The medical part of the work is invaluable."—*Calcutta Guardian.*

THE MEDICAL GUIDE FOR ANGLO-INDIANS. Being a Compendium of advice to Europeans in India, relating to the Preservation and Regulation of Health. By **R. S. Mair, F.R.C.S.E.,** late Deputy Coroner of Madras. Reprinted, with numerous additions and corrections, from "The European in India."

EASTERN EXPERIENCES. By **L. Bowring, C.S.I.,** Lord Canning's Private Secretary, and for many years the Chief Commissioner of Mysore and Coorg. In 1 vol. Demy 8vo. Price 16s. Illustrated with Maps and Diagrams.

"An admirable and exhaustive geographical, political, and industrial survey."—*Athenæum.*

"This compact and methodical summary of the most authentic information relating to countries whose welfare is intimately connected with our own."—*Daily News.*

"Interesting even to the general reader, but more especially so to those who may have a special concern in that portion of our Indian Empire."—*Post.*

65, Cornhill; & 12, Paternoster Row, London.

INDIA AND THE EAST—*continued.*

TAS-HĪL UL KALĀM; OR, HINDUSTANI MADE EASY. By **Captain W. R. M. Holroyd,** Bengal Staff Corps, Director of Public Instruction, Punjab. Crown 8vo. Price 5s.

"As clear and as instructive as possible."—*Standard.*
"Contains a great deal of most necessary information, that is not to be found in any other work on the subject that has crossed our path."—*Homeward Mail.*

Second Edition.

WESTERN INDIA BEFORE AND DURING THE MUTINIES. Pictures drawn from Life. By **Major-Gen. Sir George Le Grand Jacob, K.C.S.I., C.B.** In 1 vol. Crown 8vo. Price 7s. 6d.

"The most important contribution to the history of Western India during the Mutinies which has yet, in a popular form, been made public."—*Athenæum.*
"Few men more competent than himself to speak authoritatively concerning Indian affairs."—*Standard.*

EDUCATIONAL COURSE OF SECULAR SCHOOL BOOKS FOR INDIA. Edited by **J. S. Laurie,** of the Inner Temple, Barrister-at-Law; formerly H.M. Inspector of Schools, England; Assistant Royal Commissioner, Ireland; Special Commissioner, African Settlements; Director of Public Instruction, Ceylon.

"These valuable little works will prove of real service to many of our readers, especially to those who intend entering the Civil Service of India."—*Civil Service Gazette.*

The following Works are now ready:—

	s. d.		s. d.
THE FIRST HINDUSTANI READER, stiff linen wrapper	0 6	GEOGRAPHY OF INDIA, with Maps and Historical Appendix, tracing the growth of the British Empire in Hindustan. 128 pp. Cloth	1 6
Ditto ditto strongly bound in cloth	0 9		
THE SECOND HINDUSTANI READER, stiff linen wrapper	0 6		
Ditto ditto strongly bound in cloth	0 9		

In the Press.

ELEMENTARY GEOGRAPHY OF INDIA.

FACTS AND FEATURES OF INDIAN HISTORY, in a series of alternating Reading Lessons and Memory Exercises.

EXCHANGE TABLES OF STERLING AND INDIAN RUPEE CURRENCY, UPON A NEW AND EXTENDED SYSTEM, embracing Values from One Farthing to One Hundred Thousand Pounds, and at rates progressing, in Sixteenths of a Penny, from 1s. 9d. to 2s. 3d. per Rupee. By **Donald Fraser,** Accountant to the British Indian Steam Navigation Co. Limited. Royal 8vo. Price 10s. 6d.

"The calculations must have entailed great labour on the author, but the work is one which we fancy must become a standard one in all business houses which have dealings with any country where the rupee and the English pound are standard coins of currency."—*Inverness Courier.*

BOOKS FOR THE YOUNG AND FOR LENDING LIBRARIES.

AUNT MARY'S BRAN PIE. By the Author of "St. Olave's," "When I was a Little Girl," &c. [*In the Press.*

BY STILL WATERS. A Story in One Volume. By **Edward Garrett.** [*Preparing.*

WAKING AND WORKING; OR, FROM GIRLHOOD TO WOMANHOOD. By **Mrs. G. S. Reaney.** 1 vol. Crown 8vo. Illustrated. [*Preparing.*

PRETTY LESSONS IN VERSE FOR GOOD CHILDREN, with some Lessons in Latin, in Easy Rhyme. By **Sara Coleridge.** A New Edition. [*Preparing.*

NEW WORKS BY HESBA STRETTON.

CASSY. A New Story, by **Hesba Stretton.** Square crown 8vo, Illustrated, uniform with "Lost Gip." Price 1s. 6d.

THE KING'S SERVANTS. By **Hesba Stretton,** Author of "Lost Gip." Square crown 8vo, uniform with "Lost Gip." 8 Illustrations. Price 1s. 6d.
  Part I.—Faithful in Little. Part II.—Unfaithful. Part III.—Faithful in Much.

LOST GIP. By **Hesba Stretton,** Author of "Little Meg," "Alone in London." Square crown 8vo. Six Illustrations. Price 1s. 6d.
  ** *A HANDSOMELY BOUND EDITION, WITH TWELVE ILLUSTRATIONS, PRICE HALF-A-CROWN.*

DADDY'S PET. By **Mrs. Ellen Ross (Nelsie Brook).** Square crown 8vo, uniform with "Lost Gip." 6 Illustrations. Price 1s.

"We have been more than pleased with this simple bit of writing."—*Christian World.*

"Full of deep feeling and true and noble sentiment."—*Brighton Gazette.*

SEEKING HIS FORTUNE, AND OTHER STORIES. Crown 8vo. Four Illustrations. Price 3s. 6d.
  CONTENTS.—Seeking his Fortune.—Oluf and Stephanoff.—What's in a Name?—Contrast.—Onesta.

Three Works by MARTHA FARQUHARSON.

I. **ELSIE DINSMORE.** Crown 8vo. 3s. 6d.
II. **ELSIE'S GIRLHOOD.** Crown 8vo. 3s. 6d.
III. **ELSIE'S HOLIDAYS AT ROSELANDS.** Crown 8vo. 3s. 6d.

Each Story is independent and complete in itself. They are published in uniform size and price, and are elegantly bound and illustrated.

THE AFRICAN CRUISER. A Midshipman's Adventures on the West Coast. A Book for Boys. By S. **Whitchurch Sadler, R.N.**, Author of "Marshall Vavasour." Illustrations. Crown 8vo. 3s. 6d.

"A capital story of youthful adventure. . . . Sea-loving boys will find few pleasanter gift books this season than 'The African Cruiser.'"—*Hour.*

"Sea yarns have always been in favour with boys, but this, written in a brisk style by a thorough sailor, is crammed full of adventures."—*Times.*

BOOKS FOR THE YOUNG, ETC.—*continued*.

THE LITTLE WONDER-HORN. By **Jean Ingelow**. A Second Series of "*Stories told to a Child*." Fifteen Illustrations. Cloth, gilt. 3s. 6d.

"We like all the contents of the 'Little Wonder-Horn' very much."—*Athenæum*.
"We recommend it with confidence."—*Pall Mall Gazette*.

"Full of fresh and vigorous fancy: it is worthy of the author of some of the best of our modern verse."—*Standard*.

BRAVE MEN'S FOOTSTEPS. A Book of Example and Anecdote for Young People. Second Edition. By the Editor of "**Men who have Risen**." With Four Illustrations, by **C. Doyle**. 3s. 6d.

"A readable and instructive volume."—*Examiner*.
"The little volume is precisely of the stamp to win the favour of those who, in choosing a gift for a boy, would consult his moral development as well as his temporary pleasure."—*Daily Telegraph*.

PLUCKY FELLOWS. A Book for Boys. By **Stephen J. Mac Kenna**. With Six Illustrations. Second Edition. Crown 8vo. 3s. 6d.

"This is one of the very best 'Books for Boys' which have been issued this year."—*Morning Advertiser*.
"A thorough book for boys . . . written throughout in a manly straightforward manner that is sure to win the hearts of the children."—*London Society*.

GUTTA-PERCHA WILLIE, THE WORKING GENIUS. By **George Macdonald**. With Illustrations by **Arthur Hughes**. Crown 8vo. Second Edition. 3s. 6d.

"The cleverest child we know assures us she has read this story through five times. Mr. Macdonald will, we are convinced, accept that verdict upon his little work as final."—*Spectator*.

THE TRAVELLING MENAGERIE. By **Charles Camden**, Author of "Hoity Toity." Illustrated by **J. Mahoney**. Crown 8vo. 3s. 6d.

"A capital little book . . . . deserves a wide circulation among our boys and girls."—*Hour*.
"A very attractive story."—*Public Opinion*.

THE DESERT PASTOR, JEAN JAROUSSEAU. Translated from the French of **Eugene Pelletan**. By **Colonel E. P. De L'Hoste**. In fcap. 8vo, with an Engraved Frontispiece. New Edition. 3s. 6d.

"A touching record of the struggles in the cause of religious liberty of a real man."—*Graphic*.
"There is a poetical simplicity and picturesqueness; the noblest heroism; unpretentious religion; pure love, and the spectacle of a household brought up in the fear of the Lord. . . . ."—*Illustrated London News*.

THE DESERTED SHIP. A Real Story of the Atlantic. By **Cupples Howe**, Master Mariner. Illustrated by **Townley Green**. Crown 8vo. 3s. 6d.

"Curious adventures with bears, seals, and other Arctic animals, and with scarcely more human Esquimaux, form the mass of material with which the story deals, and will much interest boys who have a spice of romance in their composition."—*Courant*.

HOITY TOITY, THE GOOD LITTLE FELLOW. By **Charles Camden**. Illustrated. Crown 8vo. 3s. 6d.

"Relates very pleasantly the history of a charming little fellow who meddles always with a kindly disposition with other people's affairs and helps them to do right. There are many shrewd lessons to be picked up in this clever little story."—*Public Opinion*.

65, Cornhill; & 12, Paternoster Row, London.

BOOKS FOR THE YOUNG, ETC.—*continued.*

SLAVONIC FAIRY TALES. From Russian, Servian, Polish, and Bohemian Sources. Translated by **John T. Naaké.** Crown 8vo. Illustrated. Price 5*s.*

AT SCHOOL WITH AN OLD DRAGOON. By **Stephen J. Mac Kenna.** Crown 8vo. Six Illustrations. Price 5*s.*

"Consisting almost entirely of startling stories of military adventure ... Boys will find them sufficiently exciting reading."—*Times.*

"These yarns give some very spirited and interesting descriptions of soldiering in various parts of the world."—*Spectator.*

"Mr. Mac Kenna's former work, 'Plucky Fellows,' is already a general favourite, and those who read the stories of the Old Dragoon will find that he has still plenty of materials at hand for pleasant tales, and has lost none of his power in telling them well."—*Standard.*

FANTASTIC STORIES. Translated from the German of **Richard Leander,** by **Paulina B. Granville.** Crown 8vo. Eight full-page Illustrations, by **M. E. Fraser-Tytler.** Price 5*s.*

"Short, quaint, and, as they are fitly called, fantastic, they deal with all manner of subjects."—*Guardian.*

"'Fantastic' is certainly the right epithet to apply to some of these strange tales."—*Examiner.*

Third Edition.
STORIES IN PRECIOUS STONES. By **Helen Zimmern.** With Six Illustrations. Crown 8vo. Price 5*s.*

"A pretty little book which fanciful young persons will appreciate, and which will remind its readers of many a legend, and many an imaginary virtue attached to the gems they are so fond of wearing."—*Post.*

"A series of pretty tales which are half fantastic, half natural, and pleasantly quaint, as befits stories intended for the young."—*Daily Telegraph.*

THE GREAT DUTCH ADMIRALS. By **Jacob de Liefde.** Crown 8vo. Illustrated. Price 5*s.*

"May be recommended as a wholesome present for boys. They will find in it numerous tales of adventure."—*Athenæum.*

"A really good book."—*Standard.*
"A really excellent book."—*Spectator.*

PHANTASMION. A Fairy Romance. A new Edition. By **Sara Coleridge.** With an Introductory Preface by the **Right Hon. Lord Coleridge of Ottery S. Mary.** In 1 vol. Crown 8vo. Price 7*s.* 6*d.*

LAYS OF A KNIGHT ERRANT IN MANY LANDS. By **Major-General Sir Vincent Eyre, C.B., G.C.S.I.,** &c. Square crown 8vo. Six Illustrations. Price 7*s.* 6*d.*

Pharaoh Land.
Home Land.
Wonder Land.
Rhine Land.

BEATRICE AYLMER AND OTHER TALES. By the Author of "Brompton Rectory." 1 vol. Crown 8vo. [*Preparing.*

THE TASMANIAN LILY. By **James Bonwick.** Crown 8vo. Illustrated. Price 5*s.*

"An interesting and useful work."—*Hour.*
"The characters of the story are capitally conceived, and are full of those touches which give them a natural appearance."—*Public Opinion.*

MIKE HOWE, THE BUSHRANGER OF VAN DIEMEN'S LAND. By **James Bonwick,** Author of "The Tasmanian Lily," &c. Crown 8vo. With a Frontispiece.

"He illustrates the career of the bushranger half a century ago; and this he does in a highly creditable manner; his delineations of life in the bush are, to say the least, exquisite, and his representations of character are very marked."—*Edinburgh Courant.*

WORKS BY ALFRED TENNYSON, D.C.L.,

Poet Laureate.

THE CABINET EDITION.

Messrs. Henry S. King & Co. have the pleasure to announce that they will immediately issue an Edition of the Laureate's works, in *Ten Monthly Volumes*, foolscap 8vo, to be entitled "The Cabinet Edition," at *Half-a-Crown each*, which will contain the whole of Mr. Tennyson's works. The first volume will be illustrated by a beautiful Photographic Portrait, and subsequent Volumes will each contain a Frontispiece. They will be tastefully bound in Crimson Cloth, and will be issued in the following order :—

Vol.
1. EARLY POEMS.
2. ENGLISH IDYLLS & OTHER POEMS.
3. LOCKSLEY HALL & OTHER POEMS.
4. AYLMER'S FIELD & OTHER POEMS.
5. IDYLLS OF THE KING.

Vol.
6. IDYLLS OF THE KING.
7. IDYLL OF THE KING.
8. THE PRINCESS.
9. MAUD AND ENOCH ARDEN.
10. IN MEMORIAM.

Subscribers' names received by all Booksellers.

	PRICE.
	s. d.
POEMS. Small 8vo.	9 0
MAUD AND OTHER POEMS. Small 8vo.	5 0
THE PRINCESS. Small 8vo.	5 0
IDYLLS OF THE KING. Small 8vo.	7 0
,, ,, Collected. Small 8vo.	12 0
ENOCH ARDEN, &c. Small 8vo.	6 0
THE HOLY GRAIL, AND OTHER POEMS. Small 8vo.	7 0
GARETH AND LYNETTE. Small 8vo.	5 0
SELECTIONS FROM THE ABOVE WORKS. Square 8vo, cloth extra	5 0
SONGS FROM THE ABOVE WORKS. Square 8vo, cloth extra	5 0
IN MEMORIAM. Small 8vo.	6 0
LIBRARY EDITION OF MR. TENNYSON'S WORKS. 6 vols. Post 8vo, each	10 6
POCKET VOLUME EDITION OF MR. TENNYSON'S WORKS. 10 vols., in neat case	45 0
,, gilt edges	50 0
THE WINDOW; OR, THE SONGS OF THE WRENS. A Series of Songs. By Alfred Tennyson. With Music by Arthur Sullivan. 4to, cloth, gilt extra	21 0

65, Cornhill; & 12, Paternoster Row, London.

POETRY.

LYRICS OF LOVE, Selected and arranged from Shakspeare to Tennyson, by **W. Davenport Adams.** Fcap. 8vo. Price 3s. 6d.

"We cannot too highly commend this work, delightful in its contents and so pretty in its outward adornings."—*Standard.*

"Carefully selected and elegantly got up . . It is particularly rich in poems from living writers."—*John Bull.*

WILLIAM CULLEN BRYANT'S POEMS. Red-line Edition. Handsomely bound. With Illustrations and Portrait of the Author. Price 7s. 6d. A Cheaper Edition is also published. Price 3s. 6d.

These are the only complete English Editions sanctioned by the Author.

ENGLISH SONNETS. Collected and Arranged by **John Dennis.** Small crown 8vo. Elegantly bound. Price 3s. 6d.

"An exquisite selection, a selection which every lover of poetry will consult again and again with delight. The notes are very useful. . . . The volume is one for which

English literature owes Mr. Dennis the heartiest thanks."—*Spectator.*

"Mr. Dennis has shown great judgment in this selection."—*Saturday Review.*

Second Edition.

HOME-SONGS FOR QUIET HOURS. By the **Rev. Canon R. H. Baynes,** Editor of "English Lyrics" and "Lyra Anglicana." Handsomely printed and bound. Price 3s. 6d.

POEMS. By **Annette F. C. Knight.** Fcap. 8vo. [*Preparing.*

POEMS. By the **Rev. J. W. A. Taylor.** Fcap. 8vo. [*In the Press.*

ALEXANDER THE GREAT. A Dramatic Poem. By **Aubrey de Vere,** Author of "The Legends of St. Patrick," &c. Crown 8vo.

[*Nearly ready.*

THE DISCIPLES. A New Poem. By **Harriet Eleanor Hamilton King.** Crown 8vo. Price 7s. 6d.

ASPROMONTE, AND OTHER POEMS. Second Edition. Cloth, 4s. 6d.

"The volume is anonymous, but there is no reason for the author to be ashamed of it. The 'Poems of Italy' are evidently inspired by genuine enthusiasm in the cause espoused; and one of them, 'The

Execution of Felice Orsini,' has much poetic merit, the event celebrated being told with dramatic force."—*Athenæum.*

"The verse is fluent and free."—*Spectator.*

SONGS FOR MUSIC. By **Four Friends.** Square crown 8vo. Price 5s.

CONTAINING SONGS BY

Reginald A. Gatty. Stephen H. Gatty.
Greville J. Chester. Juliana H. Ewing.

"A charming gift-book, which will be very popular with lovers of poetry."—*John Bull.*

ROBERT BUCHANAN, THE POETICAL AND PROSE WORKS OF. Collected Edition, in 5 Vols. Vol. I. contains,—"Ballads and Romances;" "Ballads and Poems of Life," and a Portrait of the Author.

Vol. II.—"Ballads and Poems of Life;" "Allegories and Sonnets."

Vol. III.—"Cruiskeen Sonnets;" "Book of Orm;" "Political Mystics."

The Contents of the remaining Volumes will be duly announced.

THOUGHTS IN VERSE. Small crown 8vo. Price 1s. 6d.

This is a Collection of Verses expressive of religious feeling, written from a Theistic stand-point.

POETRY—*continued.*

COSMOS. A Poem. Small crown 8vo. Price 3s. 6d.
   SUBJECT.—Nature in the Past and in the Present.—Man in the Past and in the Present.—The Future.

NARCISSUS AND OTHER POEMS. By E. Carpenter. Small crown 8vo. Price 5s.
   " Displays considerable poetic force."—*Queen.*

A TALE OF THE SEA, SONNETS, AND OTHER POEMS. By James Howell. Crown 8vo. Cloth, 5s.
   "Mr. Howell has a keen perception of the beauties of nature, and a just appreciation of the charities of life.... Mr. Howell's book deserves, and will probably receive, a warm reception."—*Pall Mall Gazette.*

IMITATIONS FROM THE GERMAN OF SPITTA AND TERSTEGEN. By Lady Durand. Crown 8vo. 4s.
   "A charming little volume.... Will be a very valuable assistance to peaceful, meditative souls."—*Church Herald.*

Second Edition.
VIGNETTES IN RHYME. Collected Verses. By Austin Dobson. Crown 8vo. Price 5s.
   "Clever, clear-cut, and careful."—*Athenæum.*
   "As a writer of Vers de Société, Mr. Dobson is almost, if not quite, unrivalled."—*Examiner.*
   "Lively, innocent, elegant in expression, and graceful in fancy."—*Morning Post.*

ON VIOL AND FLUTE. A New Volume of Poems, by Edmund W. Gosse. With a Frontispiece by W. B. Scott. Crown 8vo. 5s.
   "A careful perusal of his verses will show that he is a poet.... His song has the grateful, murmuring sound which reminds one of the softness and deliciousness of summer time.... There is much that is good in the volume."—*Spectator.*

METRICAL TRANSLATIONS FROM THE GREEK AND LATIN POETS, AND OTHER POEMS. By R. B. Boswell, M.A. Oxon. Crown 8vo. 5s.

EASTERN LEGENDS AND STORIES IN ENGLISH VERSE. By Lieutenant Norton Powlett, Royal Artillery. Crown 8vo. 5s.
   "There is a rollicking sense of fun about the stories, joined to marvellous power of rhyming, and plenty of swing, which irresistibly reminds us of our old favourite."—*Graphic.*

EDITH; OR, LOVE AND LIFE IN CHESHIRE. By T. Ashe, Author of the "Sorrows of Hypsipyle," etc. Sewed. Price 6d.
   "A really fine poem, full of tender, subtle touches of feeling."—*Manchester News.*
   "Pregnant from beginning to end with the results of careful observation and imaginative power."—*Chester Chronicle.*

THE GALLERY OF PIGEONS, AND OTHER POEMS. By Theo. Marzials. Crown 8vo. 4s. 6d.
   "A conceit abounding in prettiness."—*Examiner.*
   "The rush of fresh, sparkling fancies is too rapid, too sustained, too abundant, not to be spontaneous."—*Academy.*

THE INN OF STRANGE MEETINGS, AND OTHER POEMS. By Mortimer Collins. Crown 8vo. 5s.
   "Abounding in quiet humour, in bright fancy, in sweetness and melody of expression, and, at times, in the tenderest touches of pathos."—*Graphic.*
   "Mr. Collins has an undercurrent of chivalry and romance beneath the trifling vein of good-humoured banter which is the special characteristic of his verse."—*Athenæum.*

EROS AGONISTES. By E. B. D. Crown 8vo. 3s. 6d.
   "It is not the least merit of these pages that they are everywhere illumined with moral and religious sentiment suggested, not paraded, of the brightest, purest character."—*Standard.*

CALDERON'S DRAMAS. Translated from the Spanish. By Denis Florence MacCarthy. 10s.
   "The lambent verse flows with an ease, spirit, and music perfectly natural, liberal, and harmonious."—*Spectator.*
   "It is impossible to speak too highly of this beautiful work."—*Month.*

SONGS FOR SAILORS. By Dr. W. C. Bennett. Dedicated by Special Request to H. R. H. the Duke of Edinburgh. Crown 8vo. 3s. 6d. With Steel Portrait and Illustrations.
   An Edition in Illustrated paper Covers. Price 1s.

WALLED IN, AND OTHER POEMS. By the Rev. Henry J. Bulkeley. Crown 8vo. 5s.
   "A remarkable book of genuine poetry."—*Evening Standard.*
   "Genuine power displayed."—*Examiner.*
   "Poetical feeling is manifest here, and the diction of the poem is unimpeachable."—*Pall Mall Gazette.*

POETRY—*continued*.

SONGS OF LIFE AND DEATH. By John Payne, Author of "Intaglios," "Sonnets," "The Masque of Shadows," etc. Crown 8vo. 5s.

"The art of ballad-writing has long been lost in England, and Mr. Payne may claim to be its restorer. It is a perfect delight to meet with such a ballad as 'May Margaret' in the present volume."—*Westminster Review.*

A NEW VOLUME OF SONNETS. By the Rev. C. Tennyson Turner. Crown 8vo. 4s. 6d.

"Mr. Turner is a genuine poet; his song is sweet and pure, beautiful in expression, and often subtle in thought."—*Pall Mall Gazette.*

"The light of a devout, gentle, and kindly spirit, a delicate and graceful fancy, a keen intelligence irradiates these thoughts."—*Contemporary Review.*

THE DREAM AND THE DEED, AND OTHER POEMS. By Patrick Scott, Author of "Footpaths between Two Worlds," etc. Fcap. 8vo. Cloth, 5s.

"A bitter and able satire on the vice and follies of the day, literary, social, and political."—*Standard.*

"Shows real poetic power coupled with evidences of satirical energy."—*Edinburgh Daily Review.*

GOETHE'S FAUST. A New Translation in Rime. By the Rev. C. Kegan Paul. Crown 8vo. 6s.

"His translation is the most minutely accurate that has yet been produced…"—*Examiner.*

"Mr. Paul is a zealous and a faithful interpreter."—*Saturday Review.*

SONGS OF TWO WORLDS. First Series. By a New Writer. Fcap. 8vo, cloth, 5s. Second Edition.

"These poems will assuredly take high rank among the class to which they belong."—*British Quarterly Review, April 1st.*

"No extracts could do justice to the exquisite tones, the felicitous phrasing and delicately wrought harmonies of some of these poems."—*Nonconformist.*

"A purity and delicacy of feeling like morning air."—*Graphic.*

SONGS OF TWO WORLDS. Second Series. By the Author of "Songs of Two Worlds." Crown 8vo. [*In the Press.*

THE LEGENDS OF ST. PATRICK AND OTHER POEMS. By Aubrey de Vere. Crown 8vo. 5s.

"Mr. De Vere's versification in his earlier poems is characterised by great sweetness and simplicity. He is master of his instrument, and rarely offends the ear with false notes."—*Pall Mall Gazette.*

"We have but space to commend the varied structure of his verse, the carefulness of his grammar, and his excellent English."—*Saturday Review.*

FICTION.

AILEEN FERRERS. By Susan Morley. In 2 vols. Crown 8vo, cloth. [*Immediately.*

IDOLATRY. A Romance. By Julian Hawthorne. Author of "Bressant." 2 vols. Crown 8vo, cloth.

VANESSA. By the Author of "Thomasina," "Dorothy," etc. 2 vols. Crown 8vo.

CIVIL SERVICE. By J. P. Listado. Author of "Maurice Rhynhart." 2 vols. Crown 8vo.

JUDITH GWYNNE. By Lisle Carr. In 3 vols. Crown 8vo, cloth.

TOO LATE. By Mrs. Newman. 2 vols. Crown 8vo.

LADY MORETOUN'S DAUGHTER. By Mrs. Eiloart. In 3 vols. Crown 8vo, cloth.

MARGARET AND ELIZABETH. A Story of the Sea. By Katherine Saunders, Author of "Gideon's Rock," etc. In 1 vol. Cloth, crown 8vo.

"Simply yet powerfully told…. This opening picture is so exquisitely drawn as to be a fit introduction to a story of such simple pathos and power…. A very beautiful story closes as it began, in a tender and touching picture of homely happiness."—*Pall Mall Gazette.*

FICTION—continued.

MR. CARINGTON. A Tale of Love and Conspiracy. By Robert Turner Cotton. In 3 vols. Cloth, crown 8vo.

"A novel in so many ways good, as in a fresh and elastic diction, stout unconventionality, and happy boldness of conception and execution. His novels, though free spoken, will be some of the healthiest of our day."—*Examiner.*

TWO GIRLS. By Frederick Wedmore, Author of "A Snapt Gold Ring." In 2 vols. Cloth, crown 8vo. [*Just out.*

"A carefully-written novel of character, contrasting the two heroines of one love tale, an English lady and a French actress. Cicely is charming; the introductory description of her is a good specimen of the well-balanced sketches in which the author shines."—*Athenæum.*

HEATHERGATE. In 2 vols. Crown 8vo, cloth. A Story of Scottish Life and Character. By a new Author.

"Its merit lies in the marked antithesis of strongly developed characters, in different ranks of life, and resembling each other in nothing but their marked nationality."—*Athenæum.*

THE QUEEN'S SHILLING. By Captain Arthur Griffiths, Author of "Peccavi." 2 vols.

"Every scene, character, and incident of the book are so life-like that they seem drawn from life direct."—*Pall Mall Gazette.*

MIRANDA. A Midsummer Madness. By Mortimer Collins. 3 vols.

"Not a dull page in the whole three volumes."—*Standard.*
"The work of a man who is at once a thinker and a poet."—*Hour.*

SQUIRE SILCHESTER'S WHIM. By Mortimer Collins, Author of "Marquis and Merchant," "The Princess Clarice," etc. 3 vols. Crown 8vo.

"We think it the best (story) Mr. Collins has yet written. Full of incident and adventure."—*Pall Mall Gazette.*
"So clever, so irritating, and so charming a story."—*Standard.*

THE PRINCESS CLARICE. A Story of 1871. By Mortimer Collins. 2 vols. Crown 8vo.

"Mr. Collins has produced a readable book, amusingly characteristic."—*Athenæum.*
"A bright, fresh, and original book."—*Standard.*

REGINALD BRAMBLE. A Cynic of the 19th Century. An Autobiography. 1 vol.

"There is plenty of vivacity in Mr. Bramble's narrative."—*Athenæum.*
"Written in a lively and readable style."—*Hour.*

EFFIE'S GAME; How she Lost and how she Won. By Cecil Clayton. 2 vols.

"Well written. The characters move, and act, and, above all, talk like human beings, and we have liked reading about them."—*Spectator.*

CHESTERLEIGH. By Ansley Conyers. 3 vols. Crown 8vo.

"We have gained much enjoyment from the book."—*Spectator.*

BRESSANT. A Romance. By Julian Hawthorne. 2 vols. Crown 8vo.

"One of the most powerful with which we are acquainted."—*Times.*
"We shall once more have reason to rejoice whenever we hear that a new work is coming out written by one who bears the honoured name of Hawthorne."—*Saturday Review.*

HONOR BLAKE: The Story of a Plain Woman. By Mrs. Keatinge, Author of "English Homes in India," etc. 2 vols. Crown 8vo.

"One of the best novels we have met with for some time."—*Morning Post.*
"A story which must do good to all, young and old, who read it."—*Daily News.*

OFF THE SKELLIGS. By Jean Ingelow. (Her First Romance.) In 4 vols. Crown 8vo.

"Clever and sparkling."—*Standard.*
"We read each succeeding volume with increasing interest, going almost to the point of wishing there was a fifth."—*Athenæum.*

SEETA. By Colonel Meadows Taylor, Author of "Tara," "Ralph Darnell," etc. 3 vols. Crown 8vo.

"Well told, native life is admirably described, and the petty intrigues of native rulers, and their hatred of the English mingled with fear lest the latter should eventually prove the victors, are cleverly depicted."—*Athenæum.*
"Thoroughly interesting and enjoyable reading."—*Examiner.*

WHAT 'TIS TO LOVE. By the Author of "Flora Adair," "The Value of Fosterstown." 3 vols.

Works Published by Henry S. King & Co.,

FICTION—*continued.*

HESTER MORLEY'S PROMISE. By Hesba Stretton. 3 vols.
"Much better than the average novels of the day; has much more claim to critical consideration as a piece of literary work,—very clever."—*Spectator.*
"All the characters stand out clearly and are well sustained, and the interest of the story never flags."—*Observer.*

THE DOCTOR'S DILEMMA. By Hesba Stretton, Author of "Little Meg," &c. &c. 3 vols. Crown 8vo.
"A fascinating story which scarcely flags in interest from the first page to the last."—*British Quarterly Review.*

THE ROMANTIC ANNALS OF A NAVAL FAMILY. By Mrs. Arthur Traherne. Crown 8vo. 10s. 6d.
"Some interesting letters are introduced; amongst others, several from the late King William IV."—*Spectator.*
"Well and pleasantly told."—*Evening Standard.*

THOMASINA. By the Author of "Dorothy," "De Cressy," &c. 2 vols. Crown 8vo.
"A finished and delicate cabinet picture; no line is without its purpose."—*Athenæum.*

JOHANNES OLAF. By E. de Wille. Translated by F. E. Bunnett. 3 vols. Crown 8vo.
"The art of description is fully exhibited; perception of character and capacity for delineating it are obvious; while there is great breadth and comprehensiveness in the plan of the story."—*Morning Post.*

THE STORY OF SIR EDWARD'S WIFE. By Hamilton Marshall, Author of "For Very Life." 1 vol. Crown 8vo.
"A quiet, graceful little story."—*Spectator.*
"Mr. Hamilton Marshall can tell a story closely and pleasantly."—*Pall Mall Gaz.*

HERMANN AGHA. An Eastern Narrative. By W. Gifford Palgrave. 2 vols. Crown 8vo, cloth, extra gilt. 18s.
"There is a positive fragrance as of newly-mown hay about it, as compared with the artificially perfumed passions which are detailed to us with such gusto by our ordinary novel-writers in their endless volumes."—*Observer.*

A GOOD MATCH. By Amelia Perrier, Author of "Mea Culpa." 2 vols.
"Racy and lively."—*Athenæum.*
"This clever and amusing novel."—*Pall Mall Gazette.*

LINKED AT LAST. By F. E. Bunnett. 1 vol. Crown 8vo.
"The reader who once takes it up will not be inclined to relinquish it without concluding the volume."—*Morning Post.*
"A very charming story."—*John Bull.*

THE SPINSTERS OF BLATCHINGTON. By Mar. Travers. 2 vols. Crown 8vo.
"A pretty story. Deserving of a favourable reception."—*Graphic.*
"A book of more than average merits."—*Examiner.*

PERPLEXITY. By Sydney Mostyn. 3 vols. Crown 8vo.
"Written with very considerable power, great cleverness, and sustained interest."—*Standard.*
"The literary workmanship is good, and the story forcibly and graphically told."—*Daily News.*

MEMOIRS OF MRS. LÆTITIA BOOTHBY. By William Clark Russell, Author of "The Book of Authors." Crown 8vo. 7s. 6d.
"Clever and ingenious." — *Saturday Review.*
"Very clever book."—*Guardian.*

CRUEL AS THE GRAVE. By the Countess Von Bothmer. 3 vols. Crown 8vo.
"*Jealousy is cruel as the Grave.*"
"Interesting, though somewhat tragic."—*Athenæum.*
"Agreeable, unaffected, and eminently readable."—*Daily News.*

HER TITLE OF HONOUR. By Holme Lee. Second Edition. 1 vol. Crown 8vo.
"With the interest of a pathetic story is united the value of a definite and high purpose."—*Spectator.*
"A most exquisitely written story."—*Literary Churchman.*

SEPTIMIUS. A Romance. By Nathaniel Hawthorne. Second Edition. 1 vol. Crown 8vo, cloth, extra gilt. 9s.
The *Athenæum* says that "the book is full of Hawthorne's most characteristic writing."

COL. MEADOWS TAYLOR'S INDIAN TALES.
THE CONFESSIONS OF A THUG

Is now ready, and is the Volume of A New and Cheaper Edition, in 1 vol. each, Illustrated, price 6s. It will be followed by "TARA" (now in the press) "RALPH DARNELL," and "TIPPOO SULTAN."

65, Cornhill; and 12, Paternoster Row, London.

THE CORNHILL LIBRARY OF FICTION.
3s. 6d. per Volume.

IT is intended in this Series to produce books of such merit that readers will care to preserve them on their shelves. They are well printed on good paper, handsomely bound, with a Frontispiece, and are sold at the moderate price of **3s. 6d.** each.

THE HOUSE OF RABY. By **Mrs. G. Hooper.**

A FIGHT FOR LIFE. By **Moy Thomas.**

ROBIN GRAY. By **Charles Gibbon.**

"Pure in sentiment, well written, and cleverly constructed."—*British Quarterly Review.*
"A pretty tale, prettily told."—*Athenæum.*
"A novel of tender and pathetic interest."—*Globe.*
"An unassuming, characteristic, and entertaining novel."—*John Bull.*

KITTY. By **Miss M. Betham-Edwards.**

"Lively and clever ... There is a certain dash in every description; the dialogue is bright and sparkling."—*Athenæum.*
"Very pleasant and amusing."—*Globe.*
"A charming novel."—*John Bull.*

HIRELL. By **John Saunders.**

"A powerful novel ... a tale written by a poet."—*Spectator.*
"A novel of extraordinary merit."—*Morning Post.*
"We have nothing but words of praise to offer for its style and composition."—*Examiner.*

ONE OF TWO; or, The left-handed Bride. By **J. H. Friswell.**

"Told with spirit ... the plot is skilfully made."—*Spectator.*
"Admirably narrated, and intensely interesting."—*Public Opinion.*

READY-MONEY MORTIBOY. A Matter-of-Fact Story.

"There is not a dull page in the whole story."—*Standard.*
"A very interesting and uncommon story."—*Vanity Fair.*
"One of the most remarkable novels which has appeared of late."—*Pall Mall Gazette.*

GOD'S PROVIDENCE HOUSE. By **Mrs. G. L. Banks.**

"Far above the run of common three-volume novels, evincing much literary power in not a few graphic descriptions of manners and local customs. ... A genuine sketch."—*Spectator.*
"Possesses the merit of care, industry, and local knowledge."—*Athenæum.*
"Wonderfully readable. The style is very simple and natural."—*Morning Post.*

FOR LACK OF GOLD. By **Charles Gibbon.**

"A powerfully written nervous story."—*Athenæum.*
"A piece of very genuine workmanship."—*British Quarterly Review.*
"There are few recent novels more powerful and engrossing."—*Examiner.*

ABEL DRAKE'S WIFE. By **John Saunders.**

"A striking book, clever, interesting, and original. We have seldom met with a book so thoroughly true to life, so deeply interesting in its detail, and so touching in its simple pathos."—*Athenæum.*

OTHER STANDARD NOVELS TO FOLLOW.

65, *Cornhill;* & 12, *Paternoster Row, London.*

THEOLOGICAL.

WORDS OF TRUTH AND CHEER. A Mission of Instruction and Suggestion. By the **Rev. Archer P. Gurney.** 1 vol. Crown 8vo. Price 6s. [*In the Press.*

THE GOSPEL ITS OWN WITNESS. Being the Hulsean Lectures for 1873. By the **Rev. Stanley Leathes.** 1 vol. Crown 8vo.

THE CHURCH AND THE EMPIRES: Historical Periods. By **Henry W. Wilberforce.** Preceded by a Memoir of the Author, by J. H. Newman, D.D. 1 vol. Post 8vo. Price 10s. 6d.

THE HIGHER LIFE. A New Volume by the **Rev. J. Baldwin Brown,** Author of "The Soul's Exodus," etc. 1 vol. Crown 8vo. Price 7s. 6d.

HARTHAM CONFERENCES; OR, DISCUSSIONS UPON SOME OF THE RELIGIOUS TOPICS OF THE DAY. By the **Rev. F. W. Kingsford, M.A.,** Vicar of S. Thomas's, Stamford Hill; late Chaplain H. E. I. C. (Bengal Presidency). "Audi alteram partem." Crown 8vo. Price 3s. 6d.

STUDIES IN MODERN PROBLEMS. A Series of Essays by various Writers. Edited by the **Rev. Orby Shipley, M.A.** Vol. I. Cr. 8vo. Price 5s.

CONTENTS.

Sacramental Confession. A. H. WARD, B.A.
Abolition of the 39 Articles. NICHOLAS POCOCK, M.A.
The Sanctity of Marriage. JOHN WALTER LEA, B.A.
Creation and Modern Science. GEORGE GREENWOOD, M.A.
Retreats for Persons Living in the World. T. T. CARTER, M.A.
Catholic and Protestant. EDWARD L. BLENKINSOPP, M.A.
The Bishops on Confession. THE EDITOR.

A Second Series is being published, price 6d. each part.

UNTIL THE DAY DAWN. Four Advent Lectures delivered in the Episcopal Chapel, Milverton, Warwickshire, on the Sunday Evenings during Advent, 1870. By the **Rev. Marmaduke E. Browne.** Crown 8vo. Price 2s. 6d.

"Four really original and stirring sermons."—*John Bull.*

A SCOTCH COMMUNION SUNDAY. To which are added Discourses from a Certain University City. Second Edition. By **A. K. H. B.,** Author of "The Recreations of a Country Parson." Crown 8vo. Second Edition. Price 5s.

"Some discourses are added, which are couched in language of rare power."—*John Bull.*
"Exceedingly fresh and readable."—*Glasgow News.*
"We commend this volume as full of interest to all our readers. It is written with much ability and good feeling, with excellent taste and marvellous tact."—*Church Herald.*

EVERY DAY A PORTION: Adapted from the Bible and the Prayer Book, for the Private Devotions of those living in Widowhood. Collected and Edited by the **Lady Mary Vyner.** Square crown 8vo, printed on good paper, elegantly bound. Price 5s.

"Now she that is a widow indeed, and desolate, trusteth in God."

THEOLOGICAL—*continued*.

CHURCH THOUGHT AND CHURCH WORK. Edited by the **Rev. Chas. Anderson, M.A.**, Editor of "Words and Works in a London Parish." Demy 8vo. Pp. 250. 7s. 6d. Containing Articles by the Rev. J. LL. DAVIES, J. M. CAPES, HARRY JONES, BROOKE LAMBERT, A. J. ROSS, Professor CHEETHAM, the EDITOR, and others.

Second Edition.
WORDS AND WORKS IN A LONDON PARISH. Edited by the **Rev. Charles Anderson, M.A.** Demy 8vo. 6s.

"It has an interest of its own for not a few minds, to whom the question 'Is the National Church worth preserving as such, and if so, how best increase its vital power?' is of deep and grave importance."—*Spectator*.

ESSAYS ON RELIGION AND LITERATURE. By Various Writers. Edited by the **Most Reverend Archbishop Manning**. Demy 8vo. 10s. 6d.

CONTENTS:—The Philosophy of Christianity.— Mystical Elements of Religion.— Controversy with the Agnostics.—A Reasoning Thought.—Darwinism brought to Book.—Mr. Mill on Liberty of the Press.— Christianity in relation to Society.—The Religious Condition of Germany.—The Philosophy of Bacon.—Catholic Laymen and Scholastic Philosophy.

WHY AM I A CHRISTIAN? By **Viscount Stratford de Redcliffe, P.C., K.G., G.C.B.** Crown 8vo. 3s. Third Edition.

"Has a peculiar interest, as exhibiting the convictions of an earnest, intelligent, and practical man."—*Contemporary Review*.

THEOLOGY AND MORALITY. Being Essays by the **Rev. J. Llewellyn Davies**. 1 vol. 8vo. Price 7s. 6d.

"The position taken up by Mr. Llewellyn Davies is well worth a careful survey on the part of philosophical students, for it represents the closest approximation of any theological system yet formulated to the religion of philosophy. . . . We have not space to do more with regard to the social essays of the work before us, than to testify to the kindliness of spirit, sobriety, and earnest thought by which they are uniformly characterised."—*Examiner*.

THE RECONCILIATION OF RELIGION AND SCIENCE. Being Essays by the **Rev. T. W. Fowle, M.A.** 1 vol. 8vo. 10s. 6d.

"A book which requires and deserves the respectful attention of all reflecting Churchmen. It is earnest, reverent, thoughtful, and courageous. . . . There is scarcely a page in the book which is not equally worthy of a thoughtful pause."—*Literary Churchman*.

HYMNS AND SACRED LYRICS. By the **Rev. Godfrey Thring, B.A.** 1 vol. Crown 8vo.

HYMNS AND VERSES, Original and Translated. By the **Rev. Henry Downton**. Small crown 8vo. 3s. 6d.

"Considerable force and beauty characterise some of these verses."—*Watchman*.
"Mr. Downton's 'Hymns and Verses' are worthy of all praise."—*English Churchman*.

"Will, we do not doubt, be welcome as a permanent possession to those for whom they have been composed or to whom they have been originally addressed."—*Church Herald*.

65, Cornhill; & 12, Paternoster Row, London.

THEOLOGICAL—*continued.*

MISSIONARY ENTERPRISE IN THE EAST. By the **Rev. Richard Collins.** Illustrated. Crown 8vo. 6s.

"A very graphic story told in lucid, simple, and modest style."—*English Churchman.*
"A readable and very interesting volume."—*Church Review.*
"We may judge from our own experience, no one who takes up this charming little volume will lay it down again till he has got to the last word."—*John Bull.*

MISSIONARY LIFE IN THE SOUTH SEAS. By **James Hutton.** 1 vol. Crown 8vo. [*In the Press.*

THE ETERNAL LIFE. Being Fourteen Sermons. By the **Rev. Jas. Noble Bennie, M.A.** Crown 8vo. 6s.

"The whole volume is replete with matter for thought and study."—*John Bull.*
"Mr. Bennie preaches earnestly and well."—*Literary Churchman.*
"We recommend these sermons as wholesome Sunday reading."—*English Churchman.*

THE REALM OF TRUTH. By **Miss E. T. Carne.** Crown 8vo. 5s. 6d.

"A singularly calm, thoughtful, and philosophical inquiry into what Truth is, and what its authority."—*Leeds Mercury.*
"It tells the world what it does not like to hear, but what it cannot be told too often,
that Truth is something stronger and more enduring than our little doings, and speakings, and actings."—*Literary Churchman.*

LIFE: Conferences delivered at Toulouse. By the **Rev. Père Lacordaire.** Crown 8vo. 6s.

"Let the serious reader cast his eye upon any single page in this volume, and he will find there words which will arrest his attention and give him a desire to know more of the teachings of this worthy follower of the saintly St. Dominick."—*Morning Post.*

Second Edition.

CATHOLICISM AND THE VATICAN. With a Narrative of the Old Catholic Congress at Munich. By **J. Lowry Whittle, A.M.**, Trin. Coll., Dublin. Crown 8vo. 4s. 6d.

"We may cordially recommend his book to all who wish to follow the course of the Old Catholic movement."—*Saturday Review.*

SIX PRIVY COUNCIL JUDGMENTS—1850-1872. Annotated by **W. G. Brooke, M.A.**, Barrister-at-Law. Crown 8vo. 9s.

"The volume is a valuable record of cases forming precedents for the future."—*Athenæum.*
"A very timely and important publication. It brings into one view the great judgments of the last twenty years, which will constitute the unwritten law of the English Establishment."—*British Quarterly Review.*

THE MOST COMPLETE HYMN BOOK PUBLISHED.

HYMNS FOR THE CHURCH AND HOME. Selected and Edited by the **Rev. W. Fleming Stevenson,** Author of "Praying and Working."

The Hymn-book consists of Three Parts:—I. For Public Worship.—II. For Family and Private Worship.—III. For Children: and contains Biographical Notices of nearly 300 Hymn-writers, with Notes upon their Hymns.

*** *Published in various forms and prices, the latter ranging from 8d. to 6s. Lists and full particulars will be furnished on application to the Publisher.*

THEOLOGICAL—*continued.*

WORKS BY THE REV. H. R. HAWEIS, M.A.

Sixth Edition.

THOUGHTS FOR THE TIMES. By the **Rev. H. R. Haweis, M.A.**, "Author of Music and Morals," etc. Crown 8vo. Price 7s. 6d.

"Bears marks of much originality of thought and individuality of expression."— *Pall Mall Gazette.*

"Mr. Haweis writes not only fearlessly, but with remarkable freshness and vigour. In all that he says we perceive a transparent honesty and singleness of purpose."— *Saturday Review.*

SPEECH IN SEASON. A New Volume of Sermons. By the **Rev. H. R. Haweis.** Crown 8vo. Price 9s.

UNSECTARIAN FAMILY PRAYERS, for Morning and Evening for a Week, with short selected passages from the Bible. By the **Rev. H. R. Haweis, M.A.** Square crown 8vo. Price 3s. 6d.

WORKS BY THE REV. C. J. VAUGHAN, D.D.

THE SOLIDITY OF TRUE RELIGION. [*In the Press.*]

FORGET THINE OWN PEOPLE. An Appeal for Missions. Small Crown 8vo. Price 3s. 6d.

WORDS OF HOPE FROM THE PULPIT OF THE TEMPLE CHURCH. Crown 8vo. Price 5s.

Fourth Edition.

THE YOUNG LIFE EQUIPPING ITSELF FOR GOD'S SERVICE. Being Four Sermons Preached before the University of Cambridge, in November, 1872. Crown 8vo. Price 3s. 6d.

"Has all the writer's characteristics of devotedness, purity, and high moral tone."—*London Quarterly Review.*

"As earnest, eloquent, and as liberal as everything else that he writes."—*Examiner.*

WORKS BY THE REV. G. S. DREW, M.A.,

VICAR OF TRINITY, LAMBETH.

Second Edition.

SCRIPTURE LANDS IN CONNECTION WITH THEIR HISTORY. Bevelled Boards, 8vo. Price 10s. 6d.

"Mr. Drew has invented a new method of illustrating Scripture history — from observation of the countries. Instead of narrating his travels, and referring from time to time to the facts of sacred history belonging to the different countries, he writes an outline history of the Hebrew nation from Abraham downwards, with special reference to the various points in which the geography illustrates the history. . . . He is very successful in picturing to his readers the scenes before his own mind."—*Saturday Review.*

Second Edition.

NAZARETH: ITS LIFE AND LESSONS. Second Edition. In small 8vo, cloth. Price 5s.

"We have read the volume with great interest. It is at once succinct and suggestive, reverent and ingenious, observant of small details, and yet not forgetful of great principles."—*British Quarterly Review.*

"A very reverent attempt to elicit and develop Scripture intimations respecting our Lord's thirty years' sojourn at Nazareth. The author has wrought well at the unworked mine, and has produced a very valuable series of Scripture lessons, which will be found both profitable and singularly interesting."—*Guardian.*

THE DIVINE KINGDOM ON EARTH AS IT IS IN HEAVEN. In demy 8vo, bound in cloth. Price 10s. 6d.

"Entirely valuable and satisfactory. . . . . . . There is no living divine to whom the authorship would not be a credit."—*Literary Churchman.*

"Thoughtful and eloquent. . . . Full of original thinking admirably expressed."—*British Quarterly Review.*

THEOLOGICAL—*continued*.

WORKS OF THE LATE REV. F. W. ROBERTSON.

NEW AND CHEAPER EDITIONS.

SERMONS.

Vol. I. Small crown 8vo. Price 3s. 6d.
Vol. II. Small crown 8vo. Price 3s. 6d.
Vol. III. Small crown 8vo. Price 3s. 6d.
Vol. IV. Small crown 8vo. Price 3s. 6d.

EXPOSITORY LECTURES ON ST. PAUL'S EPISTLE TO THE CORINTHIANS. Small crown 8vo. 5s.

AN ANALYSIS OF MR. TENNYSON'S "IN MEMORIAM." (Dedicated by permission to the Poet-Laureate.) Fcap. 8vo. 2s.

THE EDUCATION OF THE HUMAN RACE. Translated from the German of Gotthold Ephraim Lessing. Fcap. 8vo. 2s. 6d.

LECTURES AND ADDRESSES, WITH OTHER LITERARY REMAINS. A New Edition. With Introduction by the Rev. Stopford A. Brooke, M.A. In One Vol. Uniform with the Sermons. 5s. [*Preparing.*

A LECTURE ON FRED. W. ROBERTSON, M.A. By the Rev. F. A. Noble. Delivered before the Young Men's Christian Association of Pittsburgh, U.S. 1s. 6d.

WORKS BY THE REV. STOPFORD A. BROOKE, M.A.

Chaplain in Ordinary to Her Majesty the Queen.

THE LATE REV. F. W. ROBERTSON, M.A., LIFE AND LETTERS OF. Edited by **Stopford Brooke, M.A.**

I. In 2 vols., uniform with the Sermons. 7s. 6d.

II. Library Edition, in demy 8vo, with Two Steel Portraits. 12s.

III. A Popular Edition, in 1 vol. 6s.

THEOLOGY IN THE ENGLISH POETS. Being Lectures delivered by the Rev. Stopford A. Brooke. 9s.

Seventh Edition.

CHRIST IN MODERN LIFE. Sermons Preached in St. James's Chapel, York Street, London. Crown 8vo. 7s. 6d.

" Nobly fearless, and singularly strong. . . . carries our admiration throughout."—*British Quarterly Review.*

Second Edition.
FREEDOM IN THE CHURCH OF ENGLAND. Six Sermons suggested by the Voysey Judgment. In 1 vol. Crown 8vo, cloth. 3s. 6d.

" A very fair statement of the views in respect to freedom of thought held by the liberal party in the Church of England."—*Blackwood's Magazine.*

" Interesting and readable, and characterised by great clearness of thought, frankness of statement, and moderation of tone."—*Church Opinion.*

Seventh Edition.
SERMONS Preached in St. James's Chapel, York Street, London. Crown 8vo. 6s.

" No one who reads these sermons will wonder that Mr. Brooke is a great power in London, that his chapel is thronged, and his followers large and enthusiastic. They are fiery, energetic, impetuous sermons, rich with the treasures of a cultivated imagination."—*Guardian.*

THE LIFE AND WORK OF FREDERICK DENISON MAURICE: A Memorial Sermon. Crown 8vo, sewed. 1s.

A NEW VOLUME OF SERMONS IS IN THE PRESS.

MISCELLANEOUS.

VILLAGE HEALTH. By **Horace Swete, M.D.** [*In the Press.*

THE POPULAR EDITION OF THE DAILY NEWS' NARRATIVE OF THE ASHANTEE WAR. 1 vol. Crown 8vo.
[*In the Press.*

HAKAYET ABDULLA. A Tale of the early British Settlement in the Malaccas. By a **Native**. Translated by **John T. Thompson**. 1 vol. Post 8vo.

THE SHAKESPEARE ARGOSY: containing much of the wealth of Shakespeare's Wisdom and Wit, alphabetically arranged by **Captain A. Harcourt**. Crown 8vo. [*In the Press.*

SOCIALISM: its Nature, its Dangers, and its Remedies considered by the **Rev. M. Kaufman, B.A.** 1 vol. Crown 8vo. [*In the Press.*

CHARACTERISTICS FROM THE WRITINGS OF Dr. J. H. NEWMAN: being Selections Personal, Historical, Philosophical, and Religious; from his various Works. Arranged with the Author's personal approval. 1 vol. With a Portrait.

Second Edition.
CREMATION; THE TREATMENT OF THE BODY AFTER DEATH: with a Description of the Process and necessary Apparatus. Crown 8vo, sewed. 1s.

'ILAM EN NAS. Historical Tales and Anecdotes of the Times of the Early Khalifahs. Translated from the Arabic Originals. By **Mrs. Godfrey Clerk,** Author of "The Antipodes and Round the World." Crown 8vo. Price 7s.

"As full of valuable information as it is of amusing incident."—*Evening Standard.*
"Those who like stories full of the genuine colour and fragrance of the East should by all means read Mrs. Godfrey Clerk's volume."—*Spectator.*

THE PLACE OF THE PHYSICIAN. Being the Introductory Lecture at Guy's Hospital, 1873-74; to which is added
   ESSAYS ON THE LAW OF HUMAN LIFE AND ON THE RELATION BETWEEN ORGANIC AND INORGANIC WORLDS.
By **James Hinton,** Author of "Man and His Dwelling-Place." Crown 8vo, cloth. Price 3s. 6d.

Third Edition.
LITTLE DINNERS; HOW TO SERVE THEM WITH ELEGANCE AND ECONOMY. By **Mary Hooper,** Author of "The Handbook of the Breakfast Table." 1 vol. Crown 8vo. Price 5s.

THE PORT OF REFUGE; OR, COUNSEL AND AID TO SHIPMASTERS IN DIFFICULTY, DOUBT, OR DISTRESS. By **Manley Hopkins,** Author of "A Handbook of Average," "A Manual of Insurance," &c. Cr. 8vo. Price 6s.

SUBJECTS:—The Shipmaster's Position and Duties.—Agents and Agency.—Average.—Bottomry, and other Means of Raising Money.—The Charter-Party, and Bill-of-Lading. Stoppage in Transitu; and the Shipowner's Lien.—Collision.

MISCELLANEOUS—*continued*.

LOMBARD STREET. A Description of the Money Market. By **Walter Bagehot.** Large crown 8vo. Fourth Edition. 7s. 6d.

"Mr. Bagehot touches incidentally a hundred points connected with his subject, and pours serene white light upon them all."—*Spectator*.

"Anybody who wishes to have a clear idea of the workings of what is called the Money Market should procure a little volume which Mr. Bagehot has just published, and he will there find the whole thing in a nut-shell."—*Saturday Review*.

"Full of the most interesting economic history."—*Athenæum*.

THE ENGLISH CONSTITUTION. By **Walter Bagehot.** A New Edition, revised and corrected, with an Introductory Dissertation on recent Changes and Events. Crown 8vo. 7s. 6d.

"A pleasing and clever study on the department of higher politics."—*Guardian*.

"No writer before him had set out so clearly what the efficient part of the English Constitution really is."—*Pall Mall Gazette*.

NEWMARKET AND ARABIA; AN EXAMINATION OF THE DESCENT OF RACERS AND COURSERS. By **Roger D. Upton**, Captain late 9th Royal Lancers. Post 8vo. With Pedigrees and Coloured Frontispiece. 9s.

"It contains a good deal of truth, and it abounds with valuable suggestions."—*Saturday Review*.

"A remarkable volume. The breeder can well ponder over its pages."—*Bell's Life*.

"A thoughtful and intelligent book... A contribution to the history of the horse of remarkable interest and importance."—*Baily's Magazine*.

MOUNTAIN, MEADOW, AND MERE: a Series of Outdoor Sketches of Sport, Scenery, Adventures, and Natural History. By **G. Christopher Davies.** With 16 Illustrations by W. HARCOURT. Crown 8vo. Price 6s.

"Mr. Davies writes pleasantly, graphically, with the pen of a lover of nature, a naturalist, and a sportsman."—*Field*.

"Pervaded throughout by the graceful melody of a natural idyl, and the details of sport are subordinated to a dominating sense of the beautiful and picturesque."—*Saturday Review*.

HOW TO AMUSE AND EMPLOY OUR INVALIDS. By **Harriet Power.** Fcap. 8vo. 2s. 6d.

"A very useful little brochure... Will become a universal favourite with the class for whom it is intended, while it will afford many a useful hint to those who live with them."—*John Bull*.

REPUBLICAN SUPERSTITIONS. Illustrated by the Political History of the United States. Including a Correspondence with M. Louis Blanc. By **Moncure D. Conway.** Crown 8vo. 5s.

"A very able exposure of the most plausible fallacies of Republicanism, by a writer of remarkable vigour and purity of style."—*Standard*.

"Mr. Conway writes with ardent sincerity. He gives us some good anecdotes, and he is occasionally almost eloquent."—*Guardian*.

STREAMS FROM HIDDEN SOURCES. By **B. Montgomerie Ranking.** Crown 8vo. 6s.

"We doubt not that Mr. Ranking's enthusiasm will communicate itself to many of his readers, and induce them in like manner to follow back these streamlets to their parent river."—*Graphic*.

"The effect of reading the seven tales he presents to us is to make us wish for some seven more of the same kind."—*Pall Mall Gazette*.

GLANCES AT INNER ENGLAND. A Lecture delivered in the United States and Canada. By **Edward Jenkins, M.P.**, Author of "Ginx's Baby," &c. Crown 8vo. 5s.

MISCELLANEOUS—*continued.*

Thirty-Second Edition.
GINX'S BABY: HIS BIRTH AND OTHER MISFORTUNES.
By **Edward Jenkins.** Crown 8vo. Price 2s.

Fourteenth Thousand.
LITTLE HODGE. A Christmas Country Carol. By **Edward Jenkins,** Author of "Ginx's Baby," &c. Illustrated. Crown 8vo. 5s.
A Cheap Edition in paper covers, price 1s.

Sixth Edition.
LORD BANTAM. By **Edward Jenkins,** Author of "Ginx's Baby." Crown 8vo. Price 2s. 6d.

LUCHMEE AND DILLOO. A Story of West Indian Life. By **Edward Jenkins,** Author of "Ginx's Baby," "Little Hodge," &c. 2 vols. Demy 8vo. Illustrated. [*Preparing.*

TALES OF THE ZENANA, OR A NUWAB'S LEISURE HOURS. In 2 Vols. Crown 8vo. [*Preparing.*

PANDURANG HARI; or, MEMOIRS OF A HINDOO. A Tale of Mahratta Life sixty years ago. With a Preface by **Sir H. Bartle E. Frere,** G.C.S.I., &c. 2 vols. Crown 8vo. Price 21s.

"There is a quaintness and simplicity in the roguery of the hero that makes his life as attractive as that of Guzman d'Alfarache or Gil Blas, and so we advise our readers not to be dismayed at the length of Pandurang Hari, but to read it resolutely through. If they do this they cannot, we think, fail to be both amused and interested."—*Times.*

GIDEON'S ROCK, and other Stories. By **Katherine Saunders.** In 1 vol. Crown 8vo. Price 6s. [*Just out.*
CONTENTS.—Gideon's Rock.—Old Matthew's Puzzle.—Gentle Jack.—Uncle Ned.—The Retired Apothecary.

JOAN MERRYWEATHER, and other Stories. By **Katherine Saunders.** In 1 vol. Crown 8vo.
CONTENTS.—The Haunted Crust.—The Flower-Girl.—Joan Merryweather.—The Watchman's Story.—An Old Letter.

MODERN PARISH CHURCHES; THEIR PLAN, DESIGN, AND FURNITURE. By **J. T. Micklethwaite.** Crown 8vo. Price 7s. 6d.

LONGEVITY; THE MEANS OF PROLONGING LIFE AFTER MIDDLE AGE. By **Dr. John Gardner,** Author of "A Handbook of Domestic Medicine," &c. Small Crown 8vo.

STUDIES AND ROMANCES. By **H. Schutz Wilson.** 1 vol. Crown 8vo. Price 7s. 6d.

"Open the book, however, at what page the reader may, he will find something to amuse and instruct, and he must be very hard to please if he finds nothing to suit him, either grave or gay, stirring or romantic, in the capital stories collected in this well-got-up volume."—*John Bull.*

THE PELICAN PAPERS. Reminiscences and Remains of a Dweller in the Wilderness. By **James Ashcroft Noble.** Crown 8vo. 6s.

"Written somewhat after the fashion of Mr. Helps's 'Friends in Council.'"—*Examiner.* "Will well repay perusal by all thoughtful and intelligent readers."—*Liverpool Leader.*

MISCELLANEOUS—*continued*.

BRIEFS AND PAPERS. Being Sketches of the Bar and the Press. By **Two Idle Apprentices.** Crown 8vo. 7s. 6d.

"Written with spirit and knowledge, and give some curious glimpses into what the majority will regard as strange and unknown territories."—*Daily News*.

"This is one of the best books to while away an hour and cause a generous laugh that we have come across for a long time."—*John Bull*.

THE SECRET OF LONG LIFE. Dedicated by Special Permission to Lord St. Leonards. Third Edition. Large crown 8vo. 5s.

"A charming little volume."—*Times*.
"A very pleasant little book, cheerful, genial, scholarly."—*Spectator*.

"Entitled to the warmest admiration."—*Pall Mall Gazette*.

SOLDIERING AND SCRIBBLING. By **Archibald Forbes,** of the *Daily News*, Author of "My Experience of the War between France and Germany." Crown 8vo. 7s. 6d.

"All who open it will be inclined to read through for the varied entertainment which it affords."—*Daily News*.

"There is a good deal of instruction to outsiders touching military life, in this volume."—*Evening Standard*.

www.ingramcontent.com/pod-product-compliance
Lightning Source LLC
Chambersburg PA
CBHW020818230426
43666CB00007B/1048